LIFE SKILLS FOR BOYS

Essential Tips and Skills Every Teenage Boy Should Know!

SYDNEY HARPER

Copyright © 2024 by Sydney Harper

All rights reserved. No part of this publication may be reproduced, distributed or transmitted in any form or by any means, including photocopying, recording, or other electronic or mechanical methods, without the prior written permission of the publisher, except in the case of brief quotations embodied in critical reviews and certain other non-commercial uses permitted by copyright law.

Trademarked names appear throughout this book. Rather than use a trademark symbol with every occurrence of a trademarked name, names are used in an editorial fashion, with no intention of infringement of the respective owner's trademark. The information in this book is distributed on an "as is" basis, without warranty. Although every precaution has been taken in the preparation of this work, neither the author nor the publisher shall have any liability to any person or entity with respect to any loss or damage caused or alleged to be caused directly or indirectly by the information contained in this book.

A boy's journey to manhood isn't about never failing — it's about getting back up every time you do.

— *Steve Harvey*

Contents

Welcome to the Journey: Building Essential Skills for Life	vii
1. Personal Care and Grooming	1
2. Daily Habits for a Productive Routine	14
3. School, Homework, and Study Skills	23
4. Essential Life Skills for Home	31
5. Financial Savvy for Teens	41
6. Building Friendships and Social Skills	50
7. First Dates and Relationships	58
8. Managing Stress and Life's Challenges	68
9. Emotional Intelligence and Mental Health	76
10. Technology and Social Media Use	86
11. Driving and Car Ownership Basics	94
12. Handling Emergencies and Basic First Aid	105
Conclusion: Moving Forward with Confidence	115

Welcome to the Journey: Building Essential Skills for Life

Hey there! Welcome to *Life Skills for Boys – Essential Tips and Skills Every Teenage Boy Should Know!*

Life as a teenage boy is a unique adventure, full of exciting twists and turns, and it's a time when you'll start to see the world from your own perspective. You're learning more about who you are, what's important to you, and what kind of person you want to become. But let's face it – figuring it all out on your own can feel pretty overwhelming. This book is here to be your personal guide, a kind of toolbox filled with all the practical, useful stuff no one might have told you yet. From making a solid first impression to handling stress, managing money, and even figuring out how to cook a simple meal, this book covers the essentials to help you grow into a confident, capable, and self-assured young man.

Why put all these topics in one book? Because the truth is, life isn't just about learning one skill or doing one thing well; it's about having a whole bunch of different skills in your back pocket, ready for whatever comes your way. Each chapter in this book explores a different area of life that'll be valuable to you now as a teen and, later on, as an adult. Think of it like a toolkit that grows with you, something you can turn to for advice and tips whenever you need them. No lectures here – just clear, straightforward ideas to help you master everyday life.

Why These Life Skills Matter

Now, you might wonder, why do these skills even matter? Isn't life mostly about school, friends, and hobbies right now? And sure, those things are important. But as you start to grow older and gain independence, there are many new situations where knowing the right skills can make a big difference. For example, knowing how to handle money smartly can help you save for things you want instead of feeling broke all the time. Or learning the basics of car maintenance could save you from a breakdown or an unexpected repair bill later on. Even simple things like understanding how to manage stress or navigate relationships can make life a whole lot easier and more enjoyable.

Having these life skills under your belt is like putting on a superhero suit. They give you confidence, they help you feel prepared, and they make you ready for whatever life throws your way. And it's not about being perfect. You don't need to master everything overnight. Instead, think of these skills as tools you can reach for whenever you need them. The more you practice them, the better you'll get, and the easier things will be.

How to Use This Book

Life Skills for Boys is designed to be your guide whenever you're ready to tackle something new. The book is divided into chapters, each one focusing on an essential area of life that you'll want to feel comfortable with as you get older. You can start at the beginning and read straight through, or you can skip around to the chapters that catch your interest first. Not sure how to handle a new friendship or a relationship? Check out the chapter on friendships and dating. Need some tips on staying organized or managing schoolwork? There's a chapter on that, too. Or maybe you're curious about managing money and saving up – don't worry, I cover that here as well.

This book isn't just for reading once and putting on the shelf; it's meant to be an ongoing resource. That means you can pick it up whenever you need a refresher or if you find yourself facing a new challenge. Over time, you'll start to build up a set of skills that'll make you feel more in control, more independent, and better prepared for whatever comes your way. Whether it's learning how to cook a few basic meals or understanding how to take care of yourself mentally and emotionally, each chapter offers tools to help you grow in every area of your life.

Your Journey Ahead

Here's the thing: growing up is all about discovery. You're going to learn new things about yourself, the world, and the people around you. There'll be times when things go smoothly and times when you hit bumps along the way. That's completely normal. This guide is here to help you through those moments, giving you practical advice and ideas to make things a little easier and a lot more manageable.

By the time you're done with this book (and don't worry, you don't have to read it all at once!), you'll have a whole toolkit of skills that'll serve you for years to come. These aren't just "adult" skills; they're life skills that help you be the best version of yourself right now. You don't need to wait until you're older to be independent, to feel strong, and to have a sense of purpose. This book will help you realize that those things can start happening today.

So, are you ready? Ready to become the guy who knows how to manage his own money, make smart choices, keep himself and his surroundings in good shape, and handle life's ups and downs with confidence? This journey is yours, and each skill you pick up along the way will help you feel more prepared, more confident, and more in control. Remember, you don't have to do everything perfectly – just take it one step at a time.

This is your time to learn, grow, and take on the world with the confidence that you've got this. And whenever you need a little extra help or a quick tip, this book will be right here, ready to guide you. Welcome to the journey!

1. Personal Care and Grooming

In this chapter, I'll dive into the essentials of personal care and grooming – topics that are crucial as you navigate your teenage years. From mastering basic hygiene habits and hair care to understanding when and how to start shaving, this chapter will help you look and feel your best. I'll also tackle managing acne and other skin issues that can pop up during this time. Let's get ready to boost your confidence and take charge of your grooming routine!

1. Basic Hygiene

Good hygiene is the foundation of staying healthy, looking fresh, and feeling confident. Here, I'll cover the basics: hand hygiene, bathing and showering, and skin care. Follow these steps to start building good habits that will keep you looking and feeling your best.

Hand Hygiene

Keeping your hands clean is one of the easiest and most effective ways to prevent getting sick. Your hands touch everything throughout the day, from door handles to keyboards, and these surfaces often carry germs. When you touch your face, these germs can enter your body through your eyes, nose, or mouth.

To keep your hands clean, follow these steps:

1. Wash Your Hands Regularly: Wet your hands with clean water, apply soap, and lather up. Scrub for at least twenty seconds – singing the "ABC" song can be a fun way to time it! Cover all areas: between your fingers, under nails, and around thumbs. Rinse thoroughly, then dry with a clean towel or air dry.

2. Use Hand Sanitizer When Needed: If soap and water aren't available, hand sanitizer with at least 60% alcohol is a good alternative. Rub it over all parts of your hands until dry. Remember, sanitizer works best on clean-looking hands.

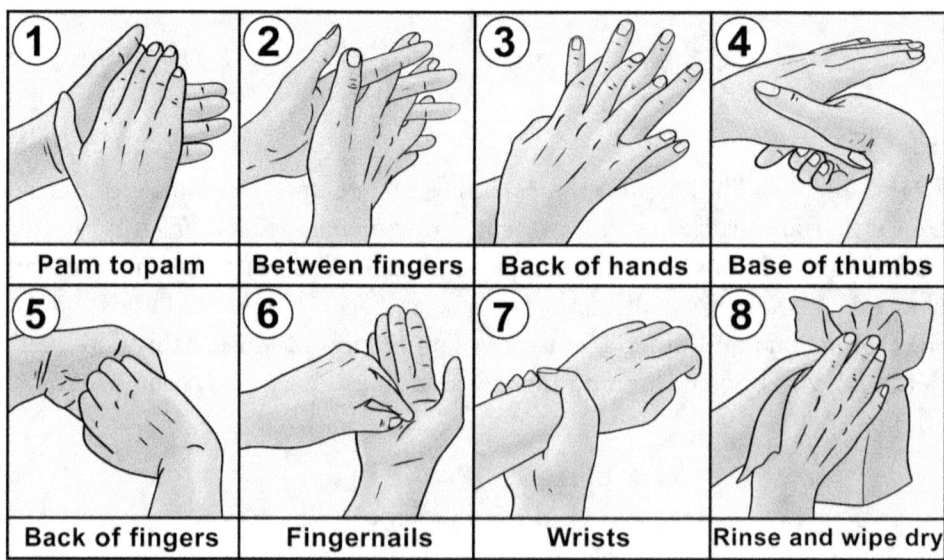

Bathing and Showering Routine

Taking a daily shower helps you feel clean, manage body odor, and maintain healthy skin. Showering every day is especially important if you're active or live in a hot climate. A five-to ten-minute shower is usually enough to cleanse without drying out your skin.

- **Choose the Right Temperature**: Warm water is best – it's effective at removing dirt and oils without drying out your skin like hot water can.
- **Use Soap or Body Wash**: Choose a product that suits your skin type (gentle, fragrance-free options are ideal for sensitive skin). If you're unsure of your skin type, see the Basic Facial Skin Care section below for tips on identifying it. Lather up your soap or body wash and focus on areas where you sweat most, like your underarms, feet, and groin, as these spots are essential for managing body odor. Make sure to rinse thoroughly to remove all product residue, which helps maintain healthy skin and prevent irritation.
- **Exfoliate Occasionally**: Gentle exfoliation removes dead skin cells to reveal smoother skin. To help keep your skin fresh through exfoliation, use a gentle scrub or exfoliating cloth once to twice a week. Avoid scrubbing too hard to prevent irritation, especially in sensitive areas.

Using Deodorant

Body odor is a natural part of growing up, especially during the teenage years when sweat glands become more active. Deodorant is a simple tool to help you stay fresh and confident throughout the day and around others. It works by reducing odor caused by bacteria on your skin, while some products labeled "antiperspirants" also minimize sweating.

Tips for Using Deodorant:

1. Apply After Showering: Put on deodorant or antiperspirant under your arms (armpits), after your shower when your skin is clean and dry. This helps it work better and last longer.

2. Choose the Right Product: Deodorants come in various forms like sprays, roll-ons, and sticks. Spray deodorants are sprayed evenly on the armpit; they dry quickly and cover large areas. Roll-ons are liquid and are applied with a rolling ball across the armpit skin. Sticks are solid and they last the longest. You apply them by rubbing a thick layer under each arm. Try a few types to see what feels and smells best for you.

3. Reapply as Needed: If you're very active or sweat a lot, reapply throughout the day to stay fresh. Keep a travel-size deodorant in your backpack or locker for quick refreshes.

Basic Facial Skin Care

Taking care of your skin is important for a healthy complexion, and knowing your skin type helps you choose the best products. There are five main skin types:

- **Normal** – Balanced, with few imperfections and no major dryness or oiliness.
- **Oily** – Often shiny with larger pores, prone to acne and blackheads.
- **Dry** – Can feel tight, with visible lines and occasional flakiness.
- **Combination** – A mix, with oiliness in the T-zone and dryness on the cheeks.
- **Sensitive** – Easily irritated, showing redness or itching

To identify your skin type, wash and leave your face product-free for a few hours, then observe if it feels oily, dry, or a mix, which will help you choose the best skincare routine.

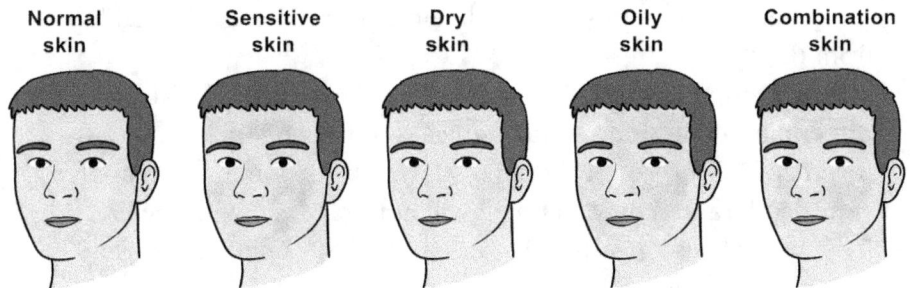

A simple but essential facial skincare routine includes:

1. Cleansing: Wash your face twice a day, morning and night, to remove dirt and oil. Use a cleanser that suits your skin type – gel or foam cleansers are ideal for oily skin as they help remove excess oil and control shine, creamy or lotion-based cleansers work well for dry skin to provide extra hydration, and gentle, fragrance-free cleansers are best for sensitive skin to avoid irritation. For combination skin, a balanced or mild foaming cleanser can be effective without drying out the skin.

2. Moisturizing: Apply a moisturizer after cleansing to lock in hydration and prevent dryness. Even if you have oily skin, don't skip this step; choose an oil-free moisturizer that keeps your skin balanced.

3. Sun Protection: Use sunscreen every day, even if it's cloudy. Pick one with SPF 30 or higher to protect against ultraviolet (UV) rays, which can cause skin damage and increase the risk of skin cancer. Reapply every two hours if you're outdoors for long periods.

These basic hygiene habits will keep you feeling clean, confident, and ready to tackle the day!

EXAMPLE SCENARIOS:

- **Showering After a Long Practice:** After an intense soccer practice, you're sweaty and exhausted, but you know that skipping a shower isn't an option. Hit the showers and use soap to wash away sweat and dirt. Besides helping you feel fresh and clean, this

quick habit also keeps your skin healthy by removing any buildup from the day.
- **Using Deodorant Before a Big Presentation:** You've got a presentation after lunch, and you want to feel confident and put-together. Right before heading to class, take a moment to reapply your deodorant. This quick step will not only keep you smelling fresh but will also give you that extra boost of confidence so you can focus on your presentation.

2. Hair Care and Styling Tips

Keeping your hair healthy and looking its best doesn't have to be complicated. Whether your hair is curly, straight, thick, or thin, a few simple routines can make a big difference. Healthy hair not only enhances your appearance but also shows that you're taking care of yourself.

Choosing the Right Product

Using the right shampoo and conditioner for your hair type is essential. If your hair is dry or coarse, try moisturizing shampoos and conditioners. If it's oily, look for balancing or clarifying products that control oil. Be careful with products containing harsh chemicals, as they can dry out or damage hair over time.

Shampooing Effectively

Shampoo is mainly for the scalp because that's where oil, sweat, and dead skin cells accumulate. By focusing on the scalp, you remove buildup and keep hair roots clean. Here's a simple step-by-step guide to shampooing effectively:

1. Wet Your Hair Thoroughly: Use warm water to fully soak your hair. This opens up the hair cuticles, allowing shampoo to lift dirt and oils.

2. Dispense Shampoo: Pour a small, quarter-sized amount of shampoo into your palm.

3. Apply to Scalp: Focus on applying shampoo to your scalp, where oil and dirt accumulate most. Gently massage it in with your fingertips (not nails) using circular motions.

4. Lather and Distribute: Work the shampoo through the roots and gently along the length of your hair. Avoid scrubbing aggressively, as this can cause tangling and breakage.

5. Rinse Thoroughly: Rinse completely to remove all residue, which can lead to buildup and dryness.

6. Repeat if Needed: If your hair is very oily or dirty, repeat the process.

Washing Routine

Overwashing can strip natural oils, leading to dryness and breakage. Try to wash your hair every two to three days to keep it clean without drying it out. Use lukewarm water instead of hot, as heat can dry and weaken your hair. On non-wash days, you can rinse your hair with water to refresh it without stripping natural oils.

Condition Properly

Conditioner keeps hair smooth and manageable, especially longer hair. After washing, apply conditioner mainly to the ends of your hair, where dryness usually starts. Let it sit for a few minutes before rinsing so it can hydrate and soften your hair.

Drying Techniques

Minimize the use of heat tools, like hair dryers and straighteners, to protect your hair from damage. When you do use a dryer, keep it on a low setting and hold it a few inches from your head. Air drying is even better, as it's gentler and keeps hair healthier.

Get Regular Trims

To prevent split ends and keep your hair looking fresh, aim for a trim every six to eight weeks if you have longer hair, or every four to six weeks if you have shorter hair. Regular trims maintain your style and encourage healthier growth by removing damaged ends.

Stay Hydrated and Eat Well

Healthy hair starts from within. A diet rich in vitamins, minerals, and omega-3 fatty acids (composed of foods such as leafy greens, nuts and seeds, berries, eggs, and whole grains) gives your hair strength and shine. Drinking plenty of water also helps keep your scalp and hair in top condition.

Protective Hairstyles

If you have longer hair, consider loose styles like buns or braids to prevent tangling or breaking, especially during sports or active routines.

Taking care of your hair can be simple, and these tips will keep it healthy, clean, and looking its best.

Example Scenarios:

- **Quick Refresh Before Meeting Friends:** You've been out all day, and your hair's looking a bit flat and messy before you head out to meet friends. Grab a bit of water to tame any flyaways, then run a comb through your hair to bring it back into shape. This simple touch-up will make you feel more polished and ready to hang out.
- **Getting Ready for School Photos:** School photo day is here, and you want your hair looking its best. The night before, wash your hair to make sure it's clean, and in the morning, style it with a small amount of gel or mousse. Using a bit of product will help keep your hairstyle looking fresh and natural in photos, giving you a confident look for the camera.

3. Shaving Basics: When and How to Start

Starting to shave is a big step, and it can feel a bit intimidating. Knowing when to start is all about personal choice. If you're noticing hair growth on your face, it's normal to feel ready to shave anywhere between thirteen and sixteen. Some guys want a clean-shaven look, while others like a bit of stubble – whatever works for you!

Here's a quick guide to help you get started:

1. Preparation is Key: Before shaving, soften the hair and prepare your skin. A warm shower or bath is a great way to open pores and soften hair, making it easier to shave. If you're not showering, try placing a warm, damp towel on your face for a few minutes.

2. Use a Clean, Sharp Razor: A sharp blade gives you a smoother shave and reduces the chance of cuts or irritation. Dull razors can pull on hair, causing redness and discomfort. Replace your blades every five to ten shaves to keep them sharp.

3. Shaving Cream or Gel: Apply a good amount of shaving cream or gel, which hydrates the hair and makes it easier to cut. It also creates a barrier, allowing the razor to glide smoothly over your skin and minimizing irritation. Avoid using regular soap, as it doesn't provide the same level of protection.

4. Shave with the Grain: Start by shaving in the direction of hair growth to avoid irritation and ingrown hairs. If you want a closer shave, you can carefully shave against the grain on a second pass, but go slow and use gentle strokes.

5. Aftercare: After shaving, rinse with cool water to close your pores, then apply a hydrating aftershave lotion or balm (avoid alcohol-based products, as they dry out the skin). Products with aloe are especially soothing.

Shaving can feel a bit awkward at first, but with the right techniques, you'll quickly get the hang of it – and be on your way to a smooth, irritation-free shave.

Example Scenarios:

- **First Time Shaving for a Clean Look:** You notice a few dark hairs on your chin, and you decide you want a cleaner look. You ask an older brother, your dad or an uncle for tips on how to get started. They walk you through the basics – using warm water to soften your skin, applying a gentle shaving cream, and shaving in the direction of hair growth to avoid irritation. Following these steps will give you a smooth, fresh look without any nicks.
- **Getting Rid of a Patchy Mustache Before an Event:** You're heading to a family event and notice your upper lip hair is starting to look a bit uneven. To tidy up, use a basic electric razor or a single-blade razor. Be careful and go slowly to avoid any cuts. This quick shave will leave you looking neat and feeling more confident for the big event.

4. Managing Acne and Common Skin Issues

Skin problems like acne, dryness, and oily skin are common during the teenage years, and knowing how to handle them can make a big difference. Acne, for instance, happens when hair follicles get clogged with oil and dead skin cells, leading to blackheads, whiteheads, or pimples. But that's not the only issue that can come up – dry patches, oily skin, and even rashes can appear as your body goes through changes. Here's a guide on how to handle acne and other skin concerns during your teenage years.

1. Gentle Cleansing: Washing your face twice a day (morning and night) with a mild, non-comedogenic cleanser (a type of facial wash designed not to clog pores) is the foundation of any good skincare routine. Use lukewarm water and your fingertips to gently massage the cleanser into your skin, then rinse thoroughly. This simple step helps remove excess oil and dirt that can clog pores and lead to breakouts.

2. Topical Treatments for Acne: For acne-prone skin, over-the-counter treatments containing benzoyl peroxide or salicylic acid can help by reducing oil production and fighting acne-causing bacteria. Start by applying these products to areas prone to breakouts (forehead, nose, and chin) once a day, preferably in the evening, to see how your skin reacts. If your skin tolerates it well without excessive dryness or irritation, you can gradually increase to applying it twice a day (morning and evening). Be consistent, as it can take a few weeks to see results. For more severe cases, consult a dermatologist who can suggest stronger prescription options.

3. Moisturize Regularly: It's a common myth that acne-prone or oily skin doesn't need moisturizer, but in reality, all skin types benefit from hydration. Use a non-comedogenic (non-pore-clogging) moisturizer daily to help maintain balance, especially if you're using acne treatments that can dry out your skin.

4. Avoid Touching or Picking at Skin: Whether dealing with acne, dry patches, or rashes, resist the urge to touch or pick at your skin. Touching can introduce bacteria, which makes breakouts worse, and picking can cause scarring. Keeping your hands off your face helps reduce the spread of bacteria and prevents further irritation.

5. Be Mindful of Diet: What you eat can impact your skin. Some studies suggest that certain foods – like sugary snacks, fried foods, and dairy – can contribute to acne and oily skin. Experiment by eliminating these foods for a period of six to eight weeks to see if it helps. With the skin renewal cycle taking about twenty-eight days, it can take a few weeks before you can evaluate the results of your dietary changes on your skin. Choose skin-friendly foods like fruits, veggies, and foods rich in omega-3s (like salmon and walnuts), which promote healthy skin.

6. Managing Stress for Healthier Skin: Stress has been linked to acne and other skin issues. High-stress levels can cause hormonal changes, which may lead to breakouts. Finding ways to manage stress – like through sports, meditation, or spending time with friends – can make a big difference in your skin and your mood.

7. Keep Bedding and Clothing Clean: Keeping your bedding and clothes clean is key to having clearer skin. Oils, bacteria, dandruff and dead skin cells can build up on fabrics, clogging pores and worsening acne. Changing pillowcases every few days helps, or you can rotate them: sleep on one side of a pillow the first night, flip it the next, then switch to a second pillow if available. Placing a clean T-shirt over your pillow also works. Other items like hats, hoodies or towels that come into contact with your face can also harbor oils and bacteria, so make sure to wash these regularly as well. By keeping these fabrics clean, you provide a fresh contact surface for your skin, which can go a long way in supporting a clearer complexion.

8. Stay Hydrated: Drinking plenty of water supports skin health and can indirectly help reduce acne by maintaining the skin's moisture balance, preventing excess oil that clogs pores. Hydration also aids blood flow, delivering nutrients and assisting in waste removal. While water doesn't directly "flush out toxins" that cause acne, it can help keep the skin looking clearer and reduce inflammation. Teenage boys should aim for about eight to ten cups (sixty-four to eighty ounces or two to two and half liters) of water daily. Pairing hydration with a healthy diet, good skincare, and other acne treatments is the best approach for clearer skin.

If skin problems like acne, rashes, or chronic dryness persist, consider visiting a dermatologist who can help you identify specific causes and recommend treatments tailored to your skin's needs. Taking care of your skin now can make a big difference in its health and appearance, both now and in the future.

EXAMPLE SCENARIOS:

- **Dealing with a Sudden Breakout Before a Big Event:** You have a big presentation at school coming up, and right before it, you notice a few new pimples on your face. Instead of picking at them, wash your face gently with a mild cleanser and apply a small dab of an acne spot treatment with benzoyl peroxide. This will help reduce the redness, and you'll feel more prepared and less stressed about your skin.
- **Managing Oily Skin for a Fresher Look During the Day:** You've noticed your skin gets shiny and oily by lunchtime, especially on your forehead and nose. To manage it, start carrying oil blotting sheets in your backpack. A quick blot in the restroom will keep your skin looking fresher, and you'll feel more confident as you go through the rest of your classes.

2. Daily Habits for a Productive Routine

Creating daily habits that promote a productive routine can significantly impact your life as a teenager. In this chapter, I'll explore simple yet effective practices like making your bed and decluttering your space to set a positive tone for the day. You'll learn how to establish morning and evening routines that work for you, strategies to combat procrastination, and tips for staying organized. Plus, I'll discuss the importance of setting goals and tracking your progress to help you stay focused and motivated. Let's dive in and build habits that lead to success!

1. Making Your Bed and Decluttering

Starting your day by making your bed might feel like a small, unimportant task, but it can set you up for success in ways you might not expect. A made bed doesn't just look nice – it signals to your brain that the day has begun and helps you start with a clear mind. Plus, an organized room feels much more relaxing to be in, helping you manage stress and feel more at ease. Here are some reasons why making your bed and keeping your space tidy can actually improve your day.

1. Boosts Motivation: Making your bed each morning is a quick, easy win, and that first accomplishment can boost your motivation for the day. It's a small but productive action that shows you've already completed something, helping you feel confident and ready to take on more. This little victory can encourage you to tackle other tasks, too, like studying, organizing your backpack, or planning your day.

2. Creates a Habit of Discipline: Getting into the routine of making your bed builds self-discipline and can act as a "keystone habit." This means it can set off a chain reaction of other good habits, like putting away your clothes, cleaning your desk, or keeping track of assignments. Once you start with one organized action, it's easier to stay consistent in other parts of your life.

3. Keeps Your Environment Calm: A clean, organized room is calming to walk into, especially when you're tired or have a lot of homework. Visual clutter can make you feel overwhelmed, while a tidy space helps you feel more relaxed and in control. Making your bed, along with tidying up a bit, creates a peaceful atmosphere where you can concentrate on schoolwork or just chill out.

4. Supports Better Sleep: There's nothing better than crawling into a neatly made bed after a long day. A clean and orderly bed helps your mind shift into relaxation mode, signaling to your brain that it's time to rest. Studies show that keeping a tidy sleep environment can improve sleep quality, helping you feel more rested and energized for the next day. Getting enough sleep is especially important for teenagers, who should aim for eight to ten hours per night to support growth, hormone regulation, and daily functioning. Hormone regulation during sleep can help maintain clear skin, improve mood, and support a healthy metabolism. Consistent sleep routines – going to bed and waking up at the same time – also help train your body's internal clock, making it easier to fall asleep and wake up refreshed. With consistent sleep and a tidy sleep space, you'll be setting yourself up for better health, clearer skin, and sharper focus every day.

In just a few minutes each morning, you can set yourself up for a more organized, productive, and stress-free day by making your bed and keeping clutter under control. It's a small habit with big rewards, helping you start each day with purpose and end it with a bit of calm.

Example Scenarios:

- **Starting the Day with a Quick Bed Makeover:** You wake up in a rush, but before heading to the shower, take a quick thirty seconds to pull up your blankets, fluff your pillow, and straighten out your bed. When you come back, your room will look instantly neater, and you'll feel a little more organized and ready to tackle the day.
- **Decluttering Your Desk for a Fresh Study Space:** You notice that your desk is piling up with papers, old pens, and random things that make it hard to find space to study. On a Saturday, take ten minutes to throw away old papers, put pens back in a cup, and stack your books neatly. With a cleaner space, studying will feel easier, and you'll be less distracted by the mess.

2. Morning and Evening Routines

Setting up morning and evening routines can be a powerful way to make your days run more smoothly, helping you stay organized and handle stress better. A solid routine gives you structure, helping you build positive habits that keep you on track. Here's how you can set up routines that work best for you and make your day more productive and enjoyable.

1. Kickstart Your Day with a Morning Routine: A good morning routine sets the tone for a productive day. Try starting with simple habits like making your bed, having a quick and nutritious breakfast, or doing some light exercise to wake up your body and mind. You could even set aside a couple of minutes for reflection or mindfulness to feel focused and energized. The goal is to wake up at a similar time each day and have a steady start to the day, which can boost your mood and help you feel ready to tackle what's ahead.

2. Plan Key Tasks During the Day: Once your day is going, it's helpful to schedule time blocks for your most important tasks. You could set aside time for studying, working on projects, or other priorities like hobbies or sports. Organize tasks by importance – tackling tougher ones earlier in the day can help you feel accomplished. A digital calendar or to-do list can be useful tools for keeping track of everything and checking things off as you go.

3. Don't Forget Breaks: Building short breaks into your day is key for staying motivated. After a study session or a couple of classes, a quick snack, a few minutes of stretching, or hanging out with friends can help you recharge. It's also a great time to explore hobbies you enjoy. Regular breaks prevent burnout and keep you feeling fresh.

4. End the Day with a Relaxing Night Routine: Winding down before bed is as essential as your morning routine. Choose calming activities – reading, journaling, or setting things up for the next day can all help you unwind. Try to limit screen time at least an hour before bed to improve sleep quality. Going to bed around the same time each night keeps your energy up and helps you start the next day strong.

Finding a routine that fits your style and goals – and being flexible enough to adjust it – is the key to making each day productive and balanced. Routines make life easier, help you stay organized, and ensure you have time for both studying and relaxation.

EXAMPLE SCENARIOS:

- **Starting the Day with a Consistent Morning Routine:** It's a school day, and you decide to try sticking to a simple morning routine. You set your alarm ten minutes earlier to give yourself time to wash your face, brush your teeth, and make a quick breakfast. By the time you leave, you'll feel more awake and less stressed, and it will be easier to focus at school knowing you started the day prepared.
- **Ending the Day with an Evening Routine to Wind Down:** After finishing your homework and getting ready for bed, take a

few minutes to turn off your screens, put away your phone, and do a quick check of your bag for the next day. Then, grab a book or listen to some calming music to relax. By the time you fall asleep, you'll feel less stressed and more ready to face the next day.

3. Battling Procrastination and Staying Organized

Procrastination – the habit of delaying tasks until the last minute – is one of the toughest habits to break, especially when assignments or chores feel overwhelming or boring. But putting things off usually leads to last-minute stress and hurried work, making it hard to do your best. Fortunately, there are a few simple, effective strategies you can use to help you stay on track, manage your workload, and avoid the stress that procrastination often brings.

1. Start with the Five-Minute Rule: When faced with a task you're dreading, try the five-minute rule: commit to working on it for just five minutes. Set a timer and dive in. Often, just getting started is the hardest part. Once you begin, you might find it easier to keep going. Those first few minutes can break down the mental barrier that makes tasks feel overwhelming, turning a dreaded task into something manageable.

2. Break Tasks into Small Steps: Large tasks can seem impossible to handle all at once. Breaking them down into smaller, manageable steps makes them far less intimidating. For example, if you have an essay to write, start by choosing a topic, then gather sources, and finally, tackle it one paragraph at a time. Each small task you complete builds momentum, helping you see progress without feeling swamped by the whole project.

3. Use the Pomodoro Technique: The Pomodoro Technique involves setting a timer for twenty-five minutes of focused work followed by a five-minute break. After four intervals, take a longer break to recharge. This method is great for keeping your focus while giving you a reward – short breaks – to look forward to. It helps prevent burnout by balancing periods of concentration with rest.

4. Reward Yourself for Progress: To make tasks more appealing, set small rewards for yourself. It could be anything you enjoy, like a snack, a quick video, or a game break. Knowing you'll get a treat after finishing a section of your work can make starting and completing tasks more enjoyable.

By using these strategies, you'll be better equipped to manage your time, reduce procrastination, and stay organized. As you develop these habits, you'll find it easier to stay on top of schoolwork and other responsibilities without feeling stressed or rushed.

EXAMPLE SCENARIOS:

- **Breaking a Big Assignment into Smaller Tasks:** You're assigned a big history project due in two weeks, and the thought of it feels overwhelming. Instead of waiting until the last minute, break it down into smaller tasks. Spend the first few days gathering research, then work on an outline. Next, spend a little time each day writing sections of the project. By the due date, you'll be finished and stress-free because you'll have spread the work out instead of procrastinating.
- **Staying Organized with a Simple To-Do List:** It's Monday, and you've got assignments, a sports practice, and chores to handle this week. To keep things manageable, jot down everything in a to-do list and prioritize what needs to be done first. Each time you check off a task, you'll feel more in control and motivated. By the end of the week, you'll notice you've kept on top of your work, making everything feel a little easier.

4. Setting Goals and Tracking Progress

Setting goals is one of the best ways to push yourself toward personal growth and success. Goals provide direction, focus, and motivation, whether you want to improve your grades, build a new habit, or develop a specific skill. Clear, achievable goals can help you stay on track, overcome challenges, and accomplish what matters most. Here's a guide to creating strong goals, along with some tips for sticking to them.

Choosing the Right Goal

The first step in goal-setting is identifying what you truly want to achieve. Think about what excites and interests you. What are your passions? If you're unsure, consider activities that make you lose track of time or topics you keep coming back to – these are often tied to things that you'll enjoy working toward. Next, think about your strengths. What skills or qualities do you naturally excel in? Building goals around these strengths can give you a better chance of success.

Finally, assess the opportunities around you. For example, if you're interested in sports, look into sports teams, training programs, or resources available to you. When your goal aligns with your passions, strengths, and the resources at hand, you'll be more likely to stay committed.

Making Your Goal SMART

To set a goal that's clear and achievable, try using the SMART framework, which stands for Specific, Measurable, Achievable, Relevant, and Time-bound. Let's break down what each of these means:

- **Specific**: Clearly define what you want to achieve. Instead of saying "I want to get better at math," try "I want to raise my math grade by mastering algebra concepts."
- **Measurable**: Make sure there's a way to track your progress. For instance "I will improve by scoring 90% or higher on weekly quizzes."
- **Achievable**: Set goals that are challenging but realistic. Committing to two hours of study each week is more manageable than aiming for ten hours.
- **Relevant**: Make sure your goal aligns with your bigger plans. If you hope to study engineering, improving your math grades is relevant and valuable.
- **Time-bound**: Set a deadline to keep you focused. For example, "I will reach my math grade goal by the end of the semester."

Example of a SMART Goal

Let's say you want to learn to cook some basic meals for yourself. Here's how you might turn it into a SMART goal:

- **Specific**: I want to learn how to cook five simple meals by myself.
- **Measurable**: I'll know I'm making progress when I can cook one new meal each week without help.
- **Achievable**: I'll dedicate an hour each Sunday to practicing a new recipe.
- **Relevant**: This will help me become more independent and prepare me for when I might live on my own.
- **Time-bound**: I'll reach my goal of mastering five meals in five weeks.

Tracking Your Progress

Keeping track of your progress is crucial for staying motivated and adjusting your approach when needed. Here are some tips to help:

1. Create a Checklist: Break your goal into smaller steps and check them off as you go.

2. Reflect Regularly: At the end of each week, ask yourself what went well and where you can improve.

3. Celebrate Small Wins: Reward yourself for every milestone you achieve. It could be a fun activity or a treat, but acknowledging progress will help keep you motivated.

With clear goals and regular tracking, you'll build momentum and start seeing real progress. Every step forward counts, so embrace the journey and enjoy the sense of accomplishment along the way!

EXAMPLE SCENARIOS:

- **Setting a Fitness Goal and Tracking Progress:** You want to improve your fitness and decide to start with a simple goal: running a mile without stopping. To track your progress, begin by jogging as far as you can, noting the distance and time. Each week, aim to run a little farther without taking a break. After a few weeks of consistent effort, you'll find yourself running a whole mile with ease, feeling accomplished as you see your progress.
- **Working Toward Better Grades in a Tough Subject:** Math has always been a challenge for you, and your goal this semester is to improve by at least one letter grade. To keep track of your progress, commit to studying for twenty minutes each day and getting extra help when needed. Each time you complete a quiz or test, note your score and look for areas to improve. By the end of the semester, you'll see your grades steadily rising, showing you that setting small, steady goals really pays off.

3. School, Homework, and Study Skills

School can be a challenging time, especially when it comes to balancing homework, studying, and preparing for exams. In this chapter, I'll equip you with essential skills to help you succeed academically. You'll discover effective study habits that make learning easier and tips for staying focused while tackling homework. I'll also discuss the importance of seeking help when you need it and share strategies for preparing for exams with confidence. Let's unlock your potential and make school a more manageable and rewarding experience!

1. Building Effective Study Habits

Studying effectively means learning smart ways to focus and manage time, so you can get the best results without burning out. Good study habits help you balance school work with everything else, keeping stress low and grades high. Here are some proven strategies to help you make the most of your study time.

1. Prioritize with the 80/20 Rule (Pareto Principle): The 80/20 rule says that 80% of your results come from 20% of your effort. When studying, this means focusing on the most important topics that have the biggest impact on your understanding. Instead of spending equal time on everything, identify the key areas that will help you succeed, such as core concepts or challenging topics. By concentrating on what truly matters, you'll study more efficiently.

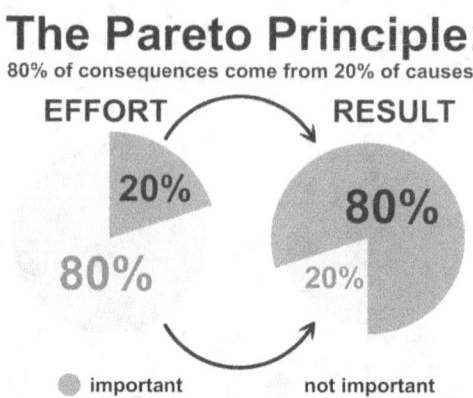

2. Use the Pomodoro Technique for Time Management: The Pomodoro Technique is a great way to stay focused. Set a timer for twenty-five minutes and work only on your study task. After twenty-five minutes, take a five-minute break. Repeat this cycle four times, then take a longer break of fifteen to thirty minutes. This method helps you maintain concentration without exhausting yourself. By regularly pausing, you keep your mind fresh and ready for the next round of studying.

3. Try Spaced Repetition for Long-Term Retention: Instead of cramming all at once, try spaced repetition. This technique involves reviewing material over increasing intervals – like studying flashcards a few days after first learning them, then again a week later. Spaced repetition strengthens your memory by revisiting information just before you're likely to forget it. Apps like Anki can help you apply this technique and build strong recall over time.

4. Create a Distraction-Free Study Environment: Where you study affects how well you focus. Pick a quiet, well-lit space, free of distractions, and have all necessary materials nearby so you don't interrupt yourself. While some people prefer complete silence, others concentrate better with instrumental music or background noise (avoid songs with lyrics as they can distract you). Experiment to find what works best for you.

5. Plan Efficiently with a Study Schedule: A study schedule helps you organize your time and prioritize tasks. Break down your homework and assign specific study blocks for each subject, especially those needing extra attention. While sticking to a schedule can help, leave some flexibility to adjust as needed.

By building these habits, you'll not only become a smarter student but also free up time to enjoy other activities, creating a balanced and productive routine!

EXAMPLE SCENARIOS:

- **Setting Up a Distraction-Free Zone:** You've noticed that it's tough to focus on homework with your phone buzzing every few minutes. To build better study habits, set up a distraction-free zone at your desk. Put your phone on silent in a drawer and keep only the materials you need on your desk. After a few days, you'll realize you're finishing assignments faster and with less stress, feeling more in control of your study time.
- **Creating a Study Schedule Before a Big Test:** With a big biology test coming up, you want to avoid last-minute cramming. You decide to break up the chapters into small sections, studying a bit each day leading up to the test. You mark off each section as you finish, keeping track of what you've already reviewed. By the time the test rolls around, you feel confident and well-prepared, knowing you've given yourself plenty of time to understand the material.

2. Tips for Homework and Staying Focused

Staying focused on homework can be challenging, especially with distractions like social media, games, and friends. But building good homework habits can save time, lower stress, and improve your grades. Here are some effective tips to help you stay on track and get things done.

1. Set a Homework Routine: Having a set time each day for homework helps your mind get into "study mode." Try working at the same time and place daily, so it becomes a regular habit. Whether it's right after school or after a short break, having a routine can make homework feel less like a chore.

2. Break Down Big Tasks: Large assignments can feel overwhelming, making it tempting to put them off. Try breaking down big projects into smaller steps. For example, if you have a paper due, start by outlining it one day, writing the introduction the next, and so on. Tackling small tasks makes the whole assignment feel more manageable.

3. Use the Five-Minute Rule: When a task seems unappealing, tell yourself you'll work on it for just five minutes. Often, once you start, it's easier to keep going. This simple rule can help you get over the initial mental block and start making progress.

4. Eliminate Distractions: Find a quiet place where you can focus without interruptions. Put your phone away or use "Do Not Disturb" mode. If you need to use a computer, avoid checking social media. Set yourself up in a place that's comfortable but not too cozy – try to avoid working on your bed, for example, so you can stay alert.

5. Take Short Breaks: Studying continuously can lead to burnout. Every twenty-five minutes, take a five-minute break to recharge (this is called the Pomodoro Technique). Go for a quick walk, stretch, or grab a snack. Short breaks keep your mind fresh and ready for more.

6. Review and Adjust Your Schedule: At the end of each week, see if there's anything you could improve about your homework time. Maybe one day you need more time for a specific subject or to prepare for a quiz. Adjusting your plan as needed keeps you organized and helps you manage your workload.

By following these tips, you'll find it easier to focus on homework, avoid procrastination, and have more free time for things you enjoy!

Example Scenarios:

- **Using a Timer to Stay on Track:** You sit down to work on a math assignment, but find yourself zoning out after a few problems. To stay focused, you decide to try the Pomodoro Technique – you set a timer for twenty-five minutes and promise yourself a five-minute break when it goes off. With the timer running, you stay focused, finishing a big part of your assignment. After a short break, you set the timer again, and soon you're done with your homework feeling accomplished and less tired.
- **Organizing Homework Tasks by Priority:** You have a few different assignments due this week, but you're not sure where to start. You list each task by its due date and difficulty level. Since a science project is due soon and will take more time, you tackle it first, breaking it down into smaller parts. After finishing the big project, you move on to the smaller assignments. By organizing and focusing on one task at a time, you avoid feeling overwhelmed and finish everything with time to spare.

3. Getting Help When You Need It

There's no shame in reaching out when you're stuck or unsure about something. Knowing when and how to ask for help is a skill that can make a huge difference in your school life and beyond. It shows self-awareness and maturity and can save you time, stress, and even grades. Here's how to ask for help effectively and make the most of it.

1. Know That It's Okay to Ask: Everyone needs help at some point, whether it's with homework, understanding a concept, or handling stress. Remind yourself that seeking assistance is normal and smart, not a weakness. If you notice others asking for help, pay attention to how it improves their work or mood – they're often better off for it.

2. Identify Exactly What You Need Help With: Before you ask, be specific about where you're struggling. Instead of saying "I don't get math," try "I'm having trouble with solving equations." This helps the person assisting you understand how they can help and shows that you've thought through the issue.

3. Choose the Right Person: Pick someone who can actually help with your problem. For school-related issues, a teacher or tutor is a good choice. For personal matters, a trusted friend or family member might be better. If you're unsure, start with someone you trust, and they can direct you to the right resources if needed.

4. Ask Respectfully and Clearly: When you reach out, be polite and get straight to the point. A simple "Could you help me understand this?" works well. Respect the other person's time, and if they're busy, ask when they might be free to help.

5. Be Open to Learning: Approach the situation with an open mind and willingness to learn. Being receptive shows maturity and encourages the person helping you to give their best advice. Plus, you'll learn faster if you're open to new ways of understanding the problem.

6. Pay It Forward: Whenever possible, help others too! It feels good to share what you know, and it creates a positive environment where everyone can learn and grow together.

By following these tips, you'll find that asking for help becomes easier and even rewarding – plus, you'll likely be able to tackle more challenges with confidence!

EXAMPLE SCENARIOS:

- **Asking a Teacher for Clarification:** In math class, you find yourself struggling with a new concept and feel unsure about the homework. Instead of trying to push through on your own, you decide to stay a few minutes after class to ask your teacher for help. They explain the steps in a simpler way and give you a few extra practice problems. With this guidance, you feel much more

confident tackling your homework and understand the concept better for the next test.
- **Reaching Out to a Friend or Study Group:** You're working on a history project but feel stuck on how to organize all the information. Remembering that a few classmates are working on the same topic, you suggest setting up a group chat to discuss ideas and share tips. During the chat, someone suggests a helpful strategy for organizing notes, and another friend shares a great online resource. By collaborating, you not only finish your project more easily but also pick up useful tips for future assignments.

4. Preparing for Exams with Confidence

Exams can feel like a lot of pressure, but preparing well can give you the confidence to tackle them without stress. Building strong study habits and a positive mindset will help you approach exams with a clear head and steady nerves. Here's a plan to prepare effectively and feel ready when exam day arrives.

1. Start Early, Don't Cram: Cramming the night before isn't helpful and usually adds more stress. Start preparing at least a week or two in advance by reviewing your notes, organizing materials, and making a study plan. Studying in smaller chunks over time helps you understand and remember information better.

2. Break Down What You Need to Know: Look at what will be covered on the exam and make a list of topics to study. Prioritize the areas you find hardest first, so you give them extra time and attention. Once you've mastered those, move on to the topics you're more comfortable with.

3. Use Practice Tests: Practice tests or past exam papers are great tools to help you understand what the actual exam will be like. They give you a feel for the question format, timing, and help you identify any weak spots. You can find many practice tests online or ask your teacher if they have old exams you can review.

4. Use the Pomodoro Technique: Studying for long hours without breaks can leave you drained and less focused. Try the Pomodoro Technique: study for twenty-five minutes, then take a five-minute break.

Repeat this a few times, then take a longer break. It keeps your mind fresh and prevents burnout.

5. Get Plenty of Rest and Fuel Up: Don't underestimate the power of sleep! A well-rested brain performs much better than a tired one. Also, eat healthy foods like fruits, nuts, and proteins – these give you energy and keep you focused.

6. Stay Positive and Visualize Success: Believe that you can succeed. Visualize yourself doing well on the exam, calmly answering questions. Positive thinking helps boost your confidence and keeps stress in check.

With these strategies, you can walk into your exams feeling prepared and self-assured, ready to do your best. Remember, your preparation will pay off, so trust yourself and give it your all!

EXAMPLE SCENARIOS:

- **Creating a Study Schedule:** You've got a big chemistry exam in two weeks, and you want to make sure you're fully prepared without feeling overwhelmed. Break down the material into sections – one section for each day – and set aside thirty minutes daily to review. By the end of the two weeks, you'll have covered everything in small, manageable chunks, which will help you walk into the exam feeling ready and calm, knowing you didn't cram at the last minute.
- **Practicing with Old Exams and Self-Quizzing:** For your English test, you decide to use some old quizzes and practice questions to test yourself. Set a timer and treat it like a real exam, aiming to work under the same conditions. After checking your answers, review any mistakes to make sure you understand them. This practice will help you feel more comfortable with the format of the test and will give you extra confidence knowing you've tackled similar questions before.

4. Essential Life Skills for Home

In this chapter, I'll dive into essential life skills that every teenage guy should know for daily life at home. From mastering laundry basics to cleaning up after meals, these skills will help you feel more independent and capable at home. I'll also cover simple ironing techniques and easy cooking tips, so you can impress your family and friends with your newfound skills. Let's get started on making your everyday home life a little easier and more enjoyable!

1. Laundry Basics

Learning how to do laundry is a key life skill that'll keep you looking sharp and feeling fresh. Understanding the basics – like sorting clothes, using the right washing techniques, and folding everything neatly – will help your clothes last longer and look their best. Here's a simple guide to mastering laundry.

Step 1: Sort Your Laundry

Sorting clothes properly before washing prevents colors from bleeding and helps delicate items stay in good shape. Start by separating clothes into three main piles:

1. **Lights**: White and light-colored clothes go in one pile to keep them bright.
2. **Darks**: Dark colors, like black, blue, and red, should be washed together to prevent dye from staining lighter clothes.
3. **Delicates and Special Fabrics**: Delicate items (like silk or wool) and heavy items (like towels or jeans) should go in separate piles to protect them from wear.

Sorting might feel like extra work, but it keeps your clothes looking fresh and helps avoid laundry disasters, like that light shirt turning a weird shade of pink!

Step 2: Check Clothing Labels

Before tossing clothes in the washer, check the tags for care instructions. Labels often indicate if a fabric needs cold water, gentle cycles, or even hand washing. Following these instructions makes a big difference in how long your clothes last.

Step 3: Use the Right Detergent and Cycle

Choose a detergent suited for your laundry needs, like one for colors or a gentler option for delicates. Here are some quick tips:

- **Cold water** is best for colors and delicates to prevent fading and shrinkage.

- **Warm water** works for lightly soiled clothes and helps dissolve dirt without being too harsh on most fabrics.
- **Heavy-duty cycles** are best for items like towels and gym clothes, but delicates should stay on a gentler cycle to avoid damage.

Step 4: Choose the Right Drying Method

Drying your clothes the right way helps prevent shrinkage and keeps fabrics looking new. Some options include:

- **Air drying**: Hang clothes on a drying rack or clothesline. This gentle method prevents shrinking and is great for delicates.
- **Dryer settings**: Use low or medium heat for synthetic fabrics and avoid high heat for items that can shrink. High heat works for towels and other durable items.

Step 5: Folding Clothes

Once your clothes are clean and dry, folding them properly saves space and keeps them wrinkle-free. Here's how to tackle different items:

1. Shirts: Lay the shirt face down, fold the sleeves across horizontally, and then fold the shirt in half vertically (or into thirds). This keeps shirts neat and compact.

2. Pants: Lay them flat, fold in half lengthwise to align the legs, and then fold up from the bottom to the waistband. Fold again if you want a smaller stack.

3. Undergarments and Socks: Fold undergarments into small squares to save space. For socks, lay one on top of the other and roll them from the toes up. This prevents the bands from stretching out and keeps pairs together.

Step 6: Organize Your Drawers

Using organizers or dividers keeps small items like socks and undergarments easy to find and neatly stored. Storing folded clothes vertically in drawers lets you see everything at a glance – no more digging to find that one favorite shirt!

Mastering laundry might seem like a small task, but it makes a big difference in your everyday routine. With these basics, you'll have clean, fresh clothes and a system that keeps your closet and drawers organized and hassle-free.

Example Scenarios:

- **Sorting Laundry by Color and Type:** You're getting ready to do your first solo laundry load, and you have both light and dark clothes. Instead of tossing everything together, separate your white T-shirts and light-colored socks from your darker items like jeans and hoodies. This way, you avoid the risk of color bleeding, keeping your clothes looking fresh and clean. Later, when you pull out your laundry, you'll see that your whites are still bright – no accidental pink T-shirts here!
- **Using the Right Amount of Detergent:** You're not sure how much detergent to add, so you check the detergent bottle label, which suggests using one capful for a regular load. Follow the instructions and measure out the recommended amount instead of guessing. Your clothes will come out clean but not overly soapy,

which would mean they need an extra rinse. Following the instructions will help you avoid detergent residue on your clothes and will save you time and water on re-rinsing!

2. Simple Ironing Tips

Ironing might seem like an extra step, but it's a skill that can make your clothes look polished and professional. Whether you have a big event, a class presentation, or just want to look sharp, learning to iron is handy. Here are some easy tips to help you iron like a pro:

1. Check the Care Label: Before ironing anything, take a look at the label on your clothing. It'll tell you which heat setting to use, whether steam is safe, or if you should avoid ironing altogether. Following these instructions prevents accidental burns or fabric damage.

2. Set Up Your Space: Prepare a clean, flat surface for ironing, ideally an ironing board. Check that the ironing board cover is smooth and stain-free. A clean setup will keep your clothes looking fresh.

3. Preheat Your Iron: Set the iron to the correct temperature based on your fabric type. Different fabrics – like cotton, wool, and polyester – need different heat settings. Let the iron fully heat up (about one to three minutes) to avoid dragging it over your clothes while it's still warming up, which can lead to wrinkles instead of removing them.

4. Use Steam and Water Sprays: Many irons have steam functions, which work great on tougher wrinkles, especially for thicker fabrics like cotton. For really stubborn creases, spray a little water directly onto the fabric before ironing. For delicate items, use steam cautiously or skip it altogether to avoid damaging the material.

5. Follow a Method: When you start ironing, work from the top of the garment downward. Start with small sections like collars, cuffs, and sleeves. Move on to larger areas like the chest or body last. For shirts and pants, iron in straight, smooth motions, and avoid scrunching up the fabric.

6. Special Fabrics and Designs: For fabrics with pleats or other details, use the tip of the iron to carefully press along the folds. For delicate materials like silk, place a cloth over the garment before ironing to prevent shiny marks.

7. Let Clothes Cool Down: After ironing, hang your clothes and let them cool for a few minutes. This helps set the press and prevents new wrinkles from forming right away.

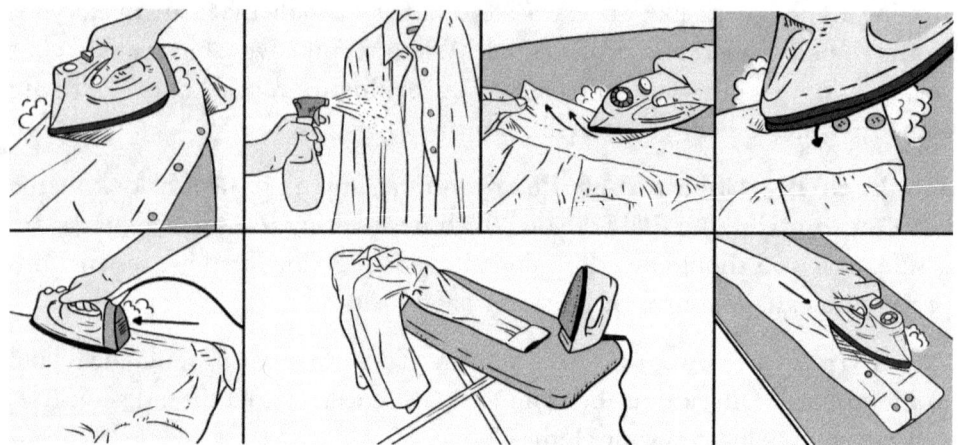

With these simple steps, you'll have wrinkle-free clothes that look sharp and professional. Ironing can feel like a chore at first, but the results make it worth the effort!

EXAMPLE SCENARIOS:

- **Getting Rid of Wrinkles for a Clean Look:** You're preparing to head out for a school event and realize your shirt is wrinkled. Instead of tossing it on and hoping no one will notice, plug in the iron, set it to the appropriate temperature for your shirt's fabric, and start with the collar. Iron each section carefully, from collar to sleeves to the main body. After a few minutes, your shirt will look crisp and neat, giving you that extra confidence boost for the event!
- **Quick Touch-Up for Last-Minute Wrinkles:** You're about to head out when you spot a few stubborn wrinkles on your pants. Instead of ironing the entire pair, give a quick steam to the wrinkled areas by hovering the iron slightly above the fabric (or, if

safe, gently pressing down). This will save you time while making your pants look smooth and tidy, so you leave looking polished without much fuss!

3. Dishwashing and Kitchen Cleanup

The kitchen is a shared space in your home and keeping it clean is key for hygiene and making mealtime more enjoyable. Knowing a few basics about washing dishes and tidying up can make this chore quick and painless. Here's how to keep your kitchen neat without too much fuss.

Step 1: Tidy as You Go

The easiest way to prevent a mess from piling up is by cleaning as you cook. After using an item, give it a quick rinse or put it directly in the dishwasher if you have one. Wiping down surfaces regularly keeps the kitchen looking fresh and saves you from a major cleanup later.

Step 2: Loading the Dishwasher

If you have a dishwasher, load it correctly to make sure all dishes get properly cleaned:

1. **Place plates, pots, and larger items** on the bottom rack, where the spray is strongest.
2. **Arrange cups, bowls, and glasses** facing downward on the top rack, so they don't fill with water.
3. **Leave space between items** for water to circulate – overcrowding leads to leftover food and spots.
4. **Run full loads** whenever possible. It's energy-efficient and saves water, but avoid packing too tightly, or some dishes won't get clean.

STEP 3: HAND-WASHING DISHES

If you're hand-washing, start by rinsing dishes under warm water to get rid of any food bits. Then, follow these tips for an effective clean:

1. **Use hot, soapy water** to kill germs and break down grease.
2. **Scrub each item well** with a sponge or dishcloth, focusing on corners and edges.
3. **Rinse with hot water** and let dishes air-dry on a rack – this is more hygienic than using a towel.

STEP 4: KEEP SUPPLIES CLEAN

Sponges and dishcloths can get gross quickly. Replace them often and microwave wet sponges for a few seconds to kill bacteria. Clean your sink regularly too, as it can collect germs and food debris.

Staying on top of dishwashing and kitchen cleanup makes the kitchen more inviting for everyone. It's a small habit that has a big impact on this shared space.

EXAMPLE SCENARIOS:

- **Cleaning Up Right After Cooking:** You've just made yourself a snack, but your dishes, utensils, and the cutting board are scattered across the counter. Instead of leaving everything for later, quickly rinse off food scraps and load what you can into the dishwasher. For hand-wash items like knives and delicate glassware, scrub them with soapy water right away and leave them to air-dry. By tidying up immediately, you avoid a messy kitchen pile-up and make your next meal prep easier!
- **Tackling Greasy Pans the Right Way:** After cooking, you notice the pan is coated in a layer of oil and food bits. Instead of scrubbing it right away and spreading the grease around, let it cool slightly, then wipe out excess grease with a paper towel. Next, soak the pan in warm, soapy water for a few minutes before scrubbing.

The pan will clean up much faster, and you'll avoid clogging the drain with grease – leaving the kitchen spotless and ready for your next cooking adventure.

4. Basic Cooking and Meal Preparation

Learning to cook is a valuable skill that'll help you eat healthier, save money, and become more independent. Plus, it's satisfying to make something tasty from scratch! Here are some basic cooking techniques to get you started with simple, delicious meals:

1. Cooking Pasta: Pasta is one of the easiest and most versatile meals to make. Start by boiling water in a large pot, adding a pinch of salt to flavor the pasta. Once the water is boiling, add your pasta and cook for around eight to twelve minutes, or until it's *al dente* (slightly firm). While the pasta cooks, sauté some onions and garlic in olive oil, then add tomato sauce, cream, or just olive oil and herbs for a quick sauce. Toss in the drained pasta, and you're ready to enjoy!

2. Making Rice: Cooking rice on the stovetop is simple once you know the trick. Use a 2:1 ratio of water to rice (e.g., two cups of water for one cup of rice). Bring the water to a boil, stir in the rice, reduce to a simmer, and cover the pot. After about twenty minutes, the rice should absorb all the water and be ready to eat. If you're lucky enough to have a rice cooker, it's even easier – just add rice and water, and let the machine handle it.

3. Boiling an Egg: Place eggs in a pot and cover them with cold water. Bring the water to a boil, then turn off the heat and cover the pot. Let the eggs sit for nine to twelve minutes, depending on how firm you like them. Transfer them to a bowl of ice water, which makes them easy to peel.

4. Making Smoothies: Smoothies are a quick, healthy snack or breakfast option. In a blender, combine your favorite fruits, a handful of greens if you like, a liquid base (like water or milk), and ice. You can also add yogurt or protein powder for extra nutrition, then blend until smooth.

5. Saving Leftovers: To avoid waste, store any leftovers in airtight containers, label with the date, and keep them in the fridge. Leftovers generally last three to four days.

Mastering these basics will help you stay energized and confident in the kitchen. With a few simple skills, you'll be able to make tasty, budget-friendly meals whenever you want!

EXAMPLE SCENARIOS:

- **Cooking a Simple Breakfast:** It's a Saturday morning, and you're feeling hungry but you don't want to eat cereal again. You decide to make scrambled eggs. You crack two eggs into a bowl, whisk them with a pinch of salt and pepper, and heat a non-stick skillet. After a few minutes, you get fluffy scrambled eggs that you can serve with toast. Not only did you prepare a tasty breakfast, but you also feel accomplished for cooking something yourself!
- **Preparing a Quick Lunch:** On a Sunday, after a busy morning of studying, it's lunchtime, and you want something satisfying. You grab some leftover grilled chicken from the fridge, chop it up, and toss it into a whole-grain wrap with lettuce, tomatoes, and a drizzle of your favorite dressing. In just a few minutes, you've created a healthy, delicious lunch that's much better than grabbing chips. Plus, you can enjoy it while catching up on your favorite show!

5. Financial Savvy for Teens

Welcome to the world of financial savvy! In this chapter, I'll equip you with the essential skills to manage your money like a pro. You'll learn how to open a bank account and navigate the basics of banking, as well as practical tips for saving and budgeting your hard-earned cash. I'll also break down credit cards and loans, helping you understand how to use them wisely. Finally, I'll tackle the important difference between needs and wants, so you can make smart money choices that set you up for success. Let's dive in and take control of your financial future!

1. Opening a Bank Account and Basic Banking

Opening a bank account is a key first step to managing your money as you start to take on more financial responsibilities. Understanding how to choose the right type of account and keep it organized will help you feel more confident and independent when handling your finances.

1. Choosing the Right Bank Account: When opening your first bank account, decide if you need a **checking** or a **savings account**. A checking account is designed for daily transactions, like spending on food or entertainment, while a savings account is great for putting money aside and may even pay interest, which means your savings could grow over time. Many banks offer special accounts for teens with no or low fees, so take a look at these options. Also, choose a bank with ATMs nearby to avoid extra fees when you need to withdraw cash.

2. Setting Up Your Account: To open a bank account, you'll usually need a few things: your personal ID (like a passport or birth certificate), proof of address, and sometimes an initial deposit. Some banks allow parents to open accounts for teens, while others will let you open your own account if you're sixteen or older. Bring everything you need and ask any questions you have – it's your money, so it's important to understand how your account works!

3. Keeping Track of Your Balance: Checking your account balance regularly is essential to avoid overspending. Most banks offer mobile apps that let you see your balance and transactions in real-time. You can even set up alerts for when your balance gets low or when money comes in and out, which helps you stay on top of your finances.

4. Learning Basic Banking Habits: Once your account is set up, get in the habit of monitoring your spending. Try these tips:

- **Track your spending** weekly so you're aware of where your money goes.
- **Set up a simple budget** for things like snacks, entertainment, and savings.
- **Avoid overdraft fees** by only spending what you have in your account.

Opening your first bank account is an exciting step toward financial independence. With a few smart habits, you'll be ready to manage your money responsibly now and build financial skills for the future.

Example Scenarios:

- **Opening Your First Bank Account:** You've just turned sixteen and want to start managing your own money. You decide to visit a local bank with a parent to open a checking account. After meeting with a bank representative, you learn about the different account options available. You choose a student account that has no monthly fees and comes with a debit card. The representative explains how to deposit money, use ATMs, and check your balance online. By the end of the visit, you feel proud to have your own account and excited to start saving for that new video game console you've been eyeing!
- **Understanding How to Use Online Banking:** A few weeks after opening your account, you want to check your balance and see how much money you have left for the month. You log into your bank's online banking app using your phone. While doing so, you discover the feature that lets you set up alerts for when your balance gets low. This way, you can better manage your spending and make sure you don't run out of money before the next allowance comes in.

2. Saving and Budgeting Tips for Teens

Learning how to save and budget your money is one of the best skills you can develop as a teenager. Saving a little now can mean big advantages down the road, whether for unexpected expenses, something you really want, or even bigger future plans.

1. Start Small, Save Regularly: Even if it feels like you don't have much money to save, start small! Set aside just a bit from any allowance, part-time job, or gift money. It's less about the amount and more about building the habit of saving. Over time, these small amounts add up and can grow significantly with interest.

2. Set Specific Goals: Saving becomes much easier when you have a goal. Think about what you want – maybe it's a new phone, a gaming console, or funds for a future trip. Break down your goals into smaller, manageable targets. For instance, if your goal costs $300, aim to save $10 a week; you'll reach your target in no time. Reaching these smaller goals keeps you motivated and on track.

3. Open a Savings Account: Having a separate savings account for your goals is a smart way to keep your savings safe from everyday spending. Look for a teen savings account with low fees and a good interest rate. Watching your money grow a little faster with interest is a good motivator to keep saving.

4. Automate Your Savings: Automating your savings makes the process super easy. If you're using a bank account, set up an automatic transfer to your savings each time you get money, like an allowance or paycheck. Some banks even have "round-up" features that round up purchases to the next dollar and put the difference into your savings account. These small deposits add up without you even noticing!

5. Build an Emergency Fund: Unexpected expenses happen. Building a small emergency fund can give you peace of mind for any surprises. Start by aiming for $100 to $500, and then, as you get older, try to build it to cover three to six months of basic expenses. This fund will be your safety net and keep you from dipping into other savings.

By practicing these budgeting and saving tips now, you'll be better prepared for managing money on your own in the future. Each small step you take now helps build a more secure financial future, so keep it up!

EXAMPLE SCENARIOS:

- **Creating a Savings Goal:** You want to buy a new skateboard that costs $150. You decide to save a portion of your weekly allowance, which is $20. You calculate how long it will take to save enough and you realize that if you save $10 each week, you'll reach your goal in fifteen weeks. With this plan, you feel motivated to stick to your savings and maybe even do extra chores for additional cash!
- **Tracking Your Spending:** You're excited to hang out with friends and want to budget for snacks and activities. To keep track, you use

a budgeting app like EveryDollar on your phone where you log your expenses. After a week, you notice you spent a lot on snacks. With the help of the app, you realize you need to cut back on impulse buys and plan ahead to save more for bigger future outings!

3. Understanding Credit Cards and Loans

Understanding credit cards and loans is key to becoming financially savvy, and learning these basics early can make a big difference. Credit cards and loans can help you pay for things you need, but they come with responsibilities and should be used wisely. A credit card allows you to borrow money from the bank up to a certain limit to make purchases, and you're expected to pay that money back – along with any interest that builds up if you don't pay off the full amount each month. When used responsibly, a credit card can help build your credit score, which is important for things like renting an apartment or applying for a loan in the future. Here's what you need to know to get started.

CHOOSING THE RIGHT CREDIT CARD

1. Research Different Cards: Look into student credit cards, which are often tailored for young people and usually offer lower credit requirements. Some may even give rewards, like cashback on school supplies or other essentials.

2. Understand the Terms: Pay attention to details like interest rates (also known as Annual Percentage Rate or APR), annual fees, and credit limits. A high APR means you'll owe more interest if you don't pay off your full balance each month. Aim for a card with no annual fee and a reasonable APR, ideally between 15% and 20%, to minimize interest costs. Compare options and choose a card that offers a competitive rate, especially if you're new to credit, to help manage expenses effectively.

3. Check Eligibility Requirements: If you're under eighteen or have no credit history, you might need a co-signer (like a parent or guardian) who would share responsibility for the card.

Applying for a Credit Card

1. Complete the Application: Fill out an application with personal details such as your Social Security number, income, and employment status. Honesty is crucial, as false information could result in denial.

2. Wait for Approval: After applying, there's a credit check. Try to avoid applying for multiple cards at once, as too many applications can lower your credit score.

Tips for Building and Maintaining a Good Credit Score

A credit score is a number that tells lenders how likely you are to repay your debts. Scores range from 300 to 850, with higher scores indicating better credit health. Here are some ways to build a good score:

1. Use Credit Wisely: Only buy what you can afford to pay off each month. Avoid letting balances carry over, as they accumulate interest and can hurt your score.

2. Pay on Time: Making payments on time is one of the biggest factors in building good credit. Consider setting up automatic payments so you're never late.

3. Monitor Credit Utilization: Aim to keep your spending under 30% of your credit limit. High usage can signal financial stress, impacting your score.

4. Check Your Score Regularly: Regularly review your credit score and report to track your progress and catch any mistakes early. Most credit card providers offer a free score check.

By learning how credit works and practicing these habits, you'll be setting yourself up for strong financial health now and in the future.

Example Scenarios:

- **Using a Credit Card Wisely:** You get your first credit card with a $500 limit and want to use it responsibly. Instead of splurging on

a new video game, you decide to use the card for necessary expenses, like gas or school supplies. By consistently paying off the balance in full each month, you'll build your credit score while avoiding interest charges and learning the importance of managing debt wisely.
- **Considering a Small Loan:** Your bike needs repairs, and you find a local shop that charges $200. You think about taking a small loan from a family member to cover the cost. Before agreeing, discuss with them how you plan to repay it, create a timeline and understand the importance of honoring your commitments. This will teach you about the responsibility that comes with borrowing money.

4. Smart Money Choices: Needs vs. Wants

One of the smartest money skills you can learn early on is knowing the difference between needs and wants. Understanding this can help you make better financial choices and keep your spending in check. Needs are essentials – things you absolutely must have, like food, clothing, school supplies, and basic personal care items. Wants, on the other hand, are things you enjoy but can live without, like video games, fast food, or the latest sneakers. The trick is learning how to balance these two categories without feeling deprived.

Tips for Separating Needs and Wants

1. Make a List: When you're about to buy something, ask yourself if it's a need or a want. Making a habit of listing out needs and wants before spending can help you think twice about impulsive purchases.

2. Set Priorities: Identify a few "wants" that matter most to you. Instead of spending on every fun item, choose a couple of things that you'll appreciate more. This way, you still enjoy your money but stay responsible.

3. Follow the 30/30/40 Rule: As a teenager, you have fewer essential needs so a simple rule for budgeting is to divide your money into 30% for needs, 30% for wants, and 40% for savings. This allows you to focus more on savings and wants:

- **30% for Essentials**: Spend 30% of your money on smaller necessities like school supplies, contributions to activities, or occasional must-haves.
- **30% for Fun or Wants**: Use 30% for personal enjoyment, such as hobbies, entertainment, or outings with friends, so you can enjoy your earnings without overspending.
- **40% for Savings**: Dedicate 40% to savings for future goals, larger purchases, or emergencies, fostering good saving habits and preparing for bigger expenses.

This split will allow you to enjoy spending money while still building strong savings habits for the future.

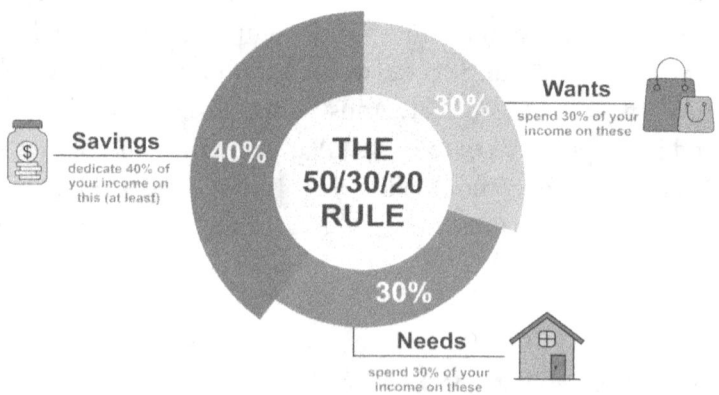

4. Delay Your Purchase: If you're tempted by a "want" item, wait a day or two. After thinking it over, you might realize it's not worth it. This helps you save money on impulse buys.

5. Use Cash: Paying with cash instead of a card can make you more aware of how much you're spending. When you physically see the money leave your hand, you might think twice about spending it on something unnecessary.

Stay Smart with Your Money

Learning to manage needs and wants is a valuable skill that will make your life easier, especially as you start earning more. By understanding these differences and following a few basic budgeting rules, you'll be able to make wise money choices without missing out on what's fun. Remember, it's about balance – making room for enjoyment while still looking out for your future.

The more you practice these strategies now, the easier it will be to handle your finances as you grow older. Smart spending isn't about saying "no" to everything; it's about knowing when to say "yes" to what really matters.

Example Scenarios:

- **Evaluating a Purchase:** You're at the mall with friends and spot a trendy pair of sneakers for $120. Before making the purchase, think about your current shoe situation. Do you really need them, or can your old pair still work for a few more months? Realizing that your current shoes are still in good shape, you choose to wait and save that money for something more essential, like school supplies or lunch for the week.
- **Planning for a Big Purchase:** You've been eyeing a new gaming console that costs $300. Instead of rushing to buy it, make a list of your monthly expenses and see if you need to prioritize things like school supplies and savings. You then decide to set aside a specific amount each week for the console, making it a goal while ensuring your essential needs are met first. This way, you learn to distinguish between what you want and what you truly need.

6. Building Friendships and Social Skills

Friendships are an important part of life, especially during your teenage years. In this chapter, I'll explore the art of building and maintaining strong friendships that can last a lifetime. You'll learn how to start conversations and engage in small talk to break the ice with new people. I'll also go over how to handle conflicts when they arise and why understanding and respecting boundaries is crucial for healthy relationships. Let's dive into the skills that will help you connect with others and create lasting bonds!

1. Building and Maintaining Friendships

Building and maintaining friendships can be one of the most rewarding parts of your teenage years. Friends are there to share good times, support you when things get tough, and make life more fun. But good friendships don't just happen – they take effort, empathy, and understanding. By learning a few key skills, you can create lasting, meaningful friendships that can be a source of joy and support throughout life.

TIPS FOR BUILDING STRONG FRIENDSHIPS

1. Be Open and Approachable: A friendly smile and a relaxed posture can go a long way. Make eye contact, and don't be afraid to start a conversation. When you're open and approachable, people will feel comfortable getting to know you.

2. Practice Active Listening: Good friends listen to each other. When your friend is talking, give them your full attention. Put your phone away, either in your pocket or your bag, so you're not tempted to look at it. Nod along, ask questions, and show that you genuinely care about what they're saying. Listening is one of the simplest ways to show respect and understanding.

3. Show Empathy: Being able to put yourself in your friend's shoes is essential. Whether they're having a tough day or celebrating a win, showing empathy strengthens your bond. A simple "I understand" or "I'm here for you" can make a big difference.

4. Be Reliable and Trustworthy: Trust is the foundation of any friendship. Keep your promises, show up when you say you will, and keep private conversations confidential. Your friends should feel they can rely on you, which is key to building a solid friendship.

5. Celebrate and Comfort: Great friends are there for the highs and the lows. Celebrate your friends' achievements – big or small – and offer a listening ear or a comforting presence during tough times. This mutual support deepens your connection.

6. Include Others and Be Kind: Friendships don't have to be exclusive. Including others in activities and being welcoming shows that you're a considerate and thoughtful friend. You never know who might bring something special to your friend group.

Nurturing Friendships Over Time

Making friends is one thing, but keeping those friendships going takes a little extra effort. Simple things like checking in with a quick message, planning to hang out on weekends, or even just chatting online can keep your friendships strong.

Friendships aren't perfect, and sometimes conflicts arise. When they do, approach the situation with an open mind and talk things out. Apologizing and forgiving can make your friendships stronger than ever.

Building lasting friendships is about being a good friend yourself. With a little empathy, reliability, and kindness, you'll create bonds that can last a lifetime.

Example Scenarios:

- **Reaching Out to a Friend:** You haven't seen your friend in a while, and you notice he seems a bit down on social media. Instead of just scrolling past, send him a quick text asking how he's doing and if he wants to hang out. This small gesture shows you care and it can help strengthen your friendship, reminding him that he has support.
- **Making Plans Together:** Your friends are planning a movie night together, but you realize you haven't seen them in a while and feel a bit left out. Instead of waiting for an invitation, suggest a game night at your place where everyone can bring their favorite snacks. This initiative will not only keep you connected but will also show that you're willing to put in the effort to maintain those friendships.

2. Starting Conversations and Small Talk

Starting conversations and making small talk may seem tricky, but with a little practice, it can become a great way to connect with people and build friendships. Whether at school, a party, or even a future job, knowing how to start and hold a conversation can make you feel more confident and approachable.

Tips for Great Small Talk

1. Be Approachable: People are more likely to talk to you if you look friendly. Keep your arms uncrossed, make eye contact, and smile! These simple body language cues show you're open to chatting and put others at ease.

2. Have Conversation Starters Ready: Sometimes, all it takes is a few simple questions or comments to get a conversation going. Here are some starters:

- **Compliments:** "I like your sneakers! Where'd you get them?"
- **Observations:** "This place is cool – have you been here before?"
- **Event-Related Questions:** "How do you know the host?" or "What do you think of the music?"
- **Personal Interests:** "What's your favorite sport?" or "Seen any good movies lately?"

3. Listen Actively: Showing interest in what the other person says keeps the conversation flowing. Nodding, smiling, and asking follow-up questions (like "What happened next?") lets them know you're really listening.

4. Share About Yourself: You don't want to make it all about the other person; sharing a bit about yourself helps balance things out. If they mention their favorite sport, you could say "I've just started playing soccer too – it's harder than it looks! Have you been playing for a long time?" Sharing helps the conversation feel natural and gives the other person a chance to relate.

5. Stick to Light Topics: Starting with easy, neutral subjects like hobbies, music, or current events keeps things comfortable. Avoid topics like politics or very personal issues until you know each other better.

6. Practice Regularly: Like any skill, the more you practice, the better you'll get. Try starting casual conversations at school, with teammates, or at family events. The more you practice, the more comfortable it becomes.

7. Know How to End the Conversation Gracefully: Wrapping up a conversation politely is just as important as starting it. Say something like "It was nice talking with you! Maybe we can catch up more at lunch sometime?" Or, if you're holding a drink, finish it and say "I'm going to grab a refill – great talking to you!"

Mastering small talk takes time, but it's worth the effort. It can make new situations feel easier, help you make friends, and build confidence in social settings. Just remember to be yourself, stay curious, and have fun with it!

EXAMPLE SCENARIOS:

- **Initiating a Chat in Class:** You sit next to a classmate you've never really talked to. Instead of just focusing on your notes, try turning to him and saying "Hey, did you understand that last topic? I thought it was a bit confusing." This opens the door for a conversation about the class where you might find out you both have similar struggles, leading to a potential study buddy situation.
- **Making Small Talk at a Party:** At a friend's birthday party, you notice someone standing alone. To break the ice, you approach him and ask "So, how do you know Jake?" This simple question can lead to a fun discussion about mutual friends or shared interests, making it easier to connect and enjoy the party together.

3. How to Handle Conflict with Friends

Conflicts with friends are bound to happen – even in the strongest friendships. Disagreements, misunderstandings, or even hurt feelings are normal parts of relationships, but handling them well can actually bring friends closer. Knowing how to apologize and work through conflicts shows maturity and respect for each other, helping you build trust and understanding.

Here's how to handle conflicts with friends:

1. Acknowledge the Mistake: If you've done something wrong, clearly own up to it. Saying something like "I know I hurt you when I said that," shows that you recognize your actions and their impact. This isn't about blaming anyone else or avoiding responsibility; it's about being honest and direct.

2. Be Sincere: A true apology comes from the heart. Avoid saying things like "I'm sorry if you felt that way," or "I'm sorry, but…" These phrases can sound like you're dismissing their feelings or making excuses. Instead, be genuine and direct: "I'm really sorry for what I said. I didn't mean to hurt you, and I feel bad about it."

3. Show Empathy: A big part of a good apology is understanding how the other person feels. Imagine how your friend must have felt in the situation, and let them know you're aware of this. Saying "I get why you were upset, and I would feel the same way if it happened to me," can show that you care about their perspective.

4. Offer to Make Amends: Actions speak louder than words. Ask if there's something you can do to make up for the mistake or avoid repeating it in the future. This step shows that you're committed to doing better and valuing their feelings.

5. Ask for Forgiveness, but Be Patient: Apologizing doesn't guarantee instant forgiveness. Sometimes people need a little time to process things, and that's okay. Let them know you hope for forgiveness, but give them space if they need it.

6. Reflect and Learn: After everything's settled, think about what you could do differently next time. Conflicts can be a learning experience, helping you become a more understanding and respectful friend.

Apologies aren't about proving who's right or wrong – they're about showing you care enough to make things right. A sincere apology can turn a conflict into a chance to grow closer and build stronger friendships.

Example Scenarios:

- **Addressing a Misunderstanding:** You and your friend had plans to hang out, but he ditched you last minute for another group. Instead of holding a grudge, you approach him the next day and say "Hey, I felt a bit left out when you canceled our plans. Can we talk about it?" By doing so, you open a dialogue, allowing both of you to express your feelings and clear the air.
- **Resolving a Disagreement:** During a group project, you and a friend disagree on the direction to take. Instead of arguing, suggest sharing other's ideas to see if you can combine them. This way, you acknowledge your friend's perspective and work together to find a solution, which helps maintain your friendship while improving teamwork.

4. Understanding and Respecting Boundaries

Understanding and respecting boundaries is a key part of building healthy friendships. Boundaries are personal limits that define what each person feels comfortable with and what feels respectful to them. Knowing these limits – and respecting them – helps you avoid misunderstandings and creates trust between you and your friends. When you respect boundaries, it shows that you value your friend's feelings and individuality.

Here's how to recognize and respect boundaries in friendships:

1. Pay Attention to Body Language: People often communicate their boundaries through body language. If a friend looks uncomfortable, pulls back, or seems uninterested, it's a sign that you might be crossing a line. For example, if they're stepping away or avoiding eye contact, it could mean they're not comfortable with the topic or activity. Respect their signals and consider adjusting your approach.

2. Ask Directly When Unsure: Sometimes, it's okay to ask what someone's boundaries are, especially if you're close friends. If you're not sure, you can ask something like "Are you okay talking about this?" or "Do you mind if we do this?" Asking shows that you care about their comfort and are willing to respect their limits.

3. Accept "No" without Pressure: If a friend says "no" to an invitation or activity, don't push them to change their mind. Pressuring someone to do something they're not comfortable with can damage trust. Accepting their "no" without questioning it shows that you respect their choices and feelings.

4. Communicate Your Own Boundaries: Boundaries go both ways! Just as it's important to respect others' boundaries, it's also important to be clear about your own. If you're uncomfortable with a situation, let your friends know politely. Saying something like "I don't really feel up for that right now," or "I'd prefer not to talk about this," helps others understand and respect your limits too.

5. Respect Personal Space and Privacy: Everyone has their own comfort level with personal space and privacy. Give your friends space when they need it, and avoid asking personal questions that might feel intrusive.

Respecting boundaries isn't about distancing yourself from others – it's about showing kindness and understanding. Healthy friendships grow when both people feel safe and respected, and understanding boundaries is a big part of that. By honoring boundaries, you create stronger, more trusting relationships that last.

EXAMPLE SCENARIOS:

- **Recognizing Personal Space:** You're hanging out with a close friend and notice that they seem uncomfortable when you lean in too close during a conversation. Instead of ignoring the vibe, you take a step back and say "Sorry if I made you uncomfortable. I won't come too close." This shows that you respect their personal space, which helps strengthen your friendship.
- **Honoring Emotional Boundaries:** Your friend shares a personal issue but seems hesitant to go into details. Rather than pressing them for more information, you respond with "I'm here for you whenever you want to talk, no pressure." This respects their emotional boundary and lets them know you care without pushing them to share more than they're ready for.

7. First Dates and Relationships

Navigating the world of first dates and relationships can be both exciting and a little nerve-wracking. In this chapter, I'll build your confidence for talking to someone new, helping you make a great first impression. You'll discover what makes a healthy relationship and learn essential dating etiquette to ensure you treat others with respect. I'll also discuss how to handle rejection gracefully, deal with breakups and understand intimacy, all skills that will serve you well in life. Let's explore the ins and outs of friendships, dating and relationships together!

1. Confidence Tips for Talking to Someone New

Feeling confident when talking to someone new can be challenging, especially if it's someone you're interested in. Confidence doesn't mean you have to be loud or the life of the party – it's about feeling comfortable with who you are. Here are some practical tips to help you feel more confident and make a good impression when meeting someone new:

1. Be Yourself: This might sound like a cliché, but it's true – authenticity is attractive. People can sense when you're trying too hard, so focus on showing up as your real self. Don't worry about impressing them with big stories or exaggerating. If they like you for who you are, that's the best kind of connection.

2. Smile and Make Eye Contact: Simple gestures like smiling and making eye contact show that you're friendly and approachable. A genuine smile can instantly make both you and the other person feel more comfortable. It's a way to say "I'm open to talking to you," without having to say a word.

3. Start with a Simple Opener: You don't need a fancy line or rehearsed phrase to start a conversation. Something as simple as "Hi, I'm [Your Name]," or "How's it going?" works just fine. If you're nervous, stick to easy, open-ended questions like "How's your day been?" or "What do you think of [something related to where you are]?"

4. Listen More Than You Talk: Confidence doesn't mean dominating the conversation. In fact, one of the best ways to connect is by listening to the other person. Nod, ask follow-up questions, and show you're interested in what they're saying. This takes the pressure off you and allows the conversation to flow naturally.

5. Stay Positive: Avoid putting yourself down or focusing on negative things. Confidence grows when you focus on the good – whether it's talking about a fun hobby or an experience you enjoyed. A positive vibe makes people want to keep talking to you.

6. Practice Makes Perfect: Talking to new people gets easier with practice. Take every chance you get to chat with classmates, teammates, or people you don't know well. Each small conversation builds your confidence and helps you feel more relaxed over time.

Remember, everyone feels nervous meeting new people, and it's okay if things don't go perfectly. What matters most is that you took the step to put yourself out there. Confidence is like a muscle – the more you use it, the stronger it gets.

EXAMPLE SCENARIOS:

- **Initiating a Conversation:** You're at a school event and notice someone sitting alone. Instead of feeling nervous, you take a deep breath and walk over, saying "Hey, I'm [Your Name]. I noticed you were sitting here alone. What do you think of the event so far?" This simple introduction opens the door for a conversation and helps you build confidence.
- **Finding Common Interests:** During lunch, you sit next to someone you don't know well. To break the ice, you ask "Have you seen any good movies lately?" When they mention a film you like, you can jump in with your thoughts. This approach shows that you're engaged and makes it easier to keep the conversation flowing, boosting your confidence as you connect over shared interests.

2. What Makes a Healthy Relationship?

Understanding what makes a healthy relationship can help you build connections that are positive, respectful, and supportive. Healthy relationships aren't about grand gestures or impressing each other – they're about honesty, communication, and mutual respect. Here are some key elements of a healthy relationship:

1. Respect: Respect is about valuing each other's opinions, interests, and boundaries. You should feel free to be yourself without fear of judgment or criticism. If your partner respects you, they'll appreciate you for who you are, not who they want you to be.

2. Open Communication: Being able to talk honestly about your feelings, boundaries, and needs is essential. Good communication means expressing yourself clearly and listening to your partner's thoughts as well. Open, respectful conversations can prevent misunderstandings and build a stronger bond.

3. Trust: Trust isn't just about loyalty – it's about feeling secure in the relationship and knowing that your partner has your back. A healthy relationship means that you both trust each other enough to share your true thoughts and feelings without fear of being judged or dismissed.

4. Boundaries and Consent: Everyone has different comfort levels. Setting and respecting boundaries is a huge part of a healthy relationship. Consent goes beyond just one aspect of a relationship; it's about checking in and making sure both people are comfortable with what's happening. Consent should be clear, enthusiastic, and ongoing – meaning it can be changed at any time, and that's okay.

5. Support: A healthy relationship should feel like a safe space where both people support each other's goals, dreams, and challenges. Your partner should encourage you to be your best self, and you should do the same for them. Whether it's cheering each other on or offering a shoulder to lean on, mutual support helps a relationship thrive.

6. Honesty: Being open and honest about your feelings, even when it's uncomfortable, builds trust. If something bothers you, don't be afraid to speak up. Healthy relationships allow for both people to express themselves without fear of a negative reaction. Honesty keeps things real and builds a deeper connection.

Remember, a healthy relationship isn't always perfect. There will be ups and downs, and that's normal. What's important is how you both handle those challenges and work through them together with respect, honesty, and a commitment to making things better.

Example Scenarios:

- **Communicating Openly:** You're hanging out with someone and notice they seem a bit off. Instead of waiting for them to say something, approach them and say "Hey, I've noticed you seem a little down today. Want to talk about it?" This shows you care and encourages open communication, which is essential for a healthy friendship or any kind of relationship.

- **Respecting Each Other's Space:** You and your friend are planning to go out, but you sense they've had a long week and might need some downtime. You say "If you're feeling tired, we can always reschedule. No pressure!" This shows you respect their feelings and need for space, which strengthens your friendship and demonstrates healthy boundaries.

3. Dating Etiquette and Respecting Boundaries

Understanding dating etiquette and respecting boundaries is essential for building respectful, enjoyable relationships. Dating isn't just about spending time with someone you like; it's about mutual respect, clear communication, and making sure both people feel comfortable and valued. Here's a guide to help you navigate dating etiquette and maintain healthy boundaries.

1. Know Your Boundaries: Before getting into a relationship, take time to think about what you're comfortable with. This could involve how much time you want to spend together, what types of activities you're comfortable with, and even how you prefer to communicate. Understanding your boundaries will make it easier to explain them clearly and confidently to your partner.

2. Communicate Early and Honestly: Don't wait until there's a problem to start talking about boundaries. Share your expectations early in the relationship. For example, if you have specific feelings about PDA (public displays of affection) or how often you'd like to text, let your partner know. Open, honest communication prevents misunderstandings and makes it clear what's okay and what isn't.

3. Respect Your Partner's Boundaries: Relationships work best when there's a balance between what each person is comfortable with. Just as you'd expect your partner to respect your boundaries, it's important to listen to and respect theirs. If they say "no" or ask for space, be understanding and supportive – it shows that you respect their needs and are willing to compromise.

4. Check In Regularly: Relationships change over time, and boundaries can too. It's good practice to occasionally check in with your partner to make sure you're both still comfortable with how things are going. You could ask "Is there anything you'd like to change or talk about?" This shows that you care about their feelings and want to keep things positive and comfortable.

5. Don't Be Afraid to Say No: Saying "no" doesn't mean you're being difficult; it means you're being honest about your needs. If you're asked to do something you're not comfortable with, it's completely okay to say "I'd rather not." A respectful partner will understand and won't pressure you.

By setting and respecting boundaries, you create a healthy foundation built on trust, respect, and understanding. Good dating etiquette isn't just about being polite – it's about ensuring that both you and your partner feel valued and safe. By following these steps, you're showing that you're considerate, thoughtful, and ready for a respectful relationship.

Example Scenarios:

- **Asking for Consent:** You're on a date, and things are going well. You want to hold your date's hand but remember the importance of consent. Instead of assuming, gently ask "Is it okay if I hold your hand?" This shows you respect your date's personal space and feelings, making them feel comfortable and valued.
- **Communicating Preferences:** You're texting someone you've been dating, and they suggest a movie night at their place. Instead of just agreeing, you respond "I'm cool with that! But can we keep it low-key, like just watch a movie and hang out?" This way, you set clear expectations about the date, respecting each other's boundaries and ensuring you're both on the same page.

4. Handling Rejection with Grace

Handling rejection is part of growing up, and although it may feel disappointing or embarrassing, knowing how to respond with grace is an important life skill. Rejection can happen in any area, whether it's romantic, social, or even on a sports team, and learning to deal with it respectfully helps build resilience and confidence.

1. Don't Take It Personally: Often, rejection has little to do with you as a person. People have their own preferences, experiences, and comfort zones, and sometimes they just aren't ready or interested. Remind yourself that being turned down doesn't define your worth or make you "less than."

2. Stay Calm and Be Respectful: In the moment, it's normal to feel hurt or frustrated, but reacting with anger or hurtful words can make the situation worse. Instead, take a deep breath and thank the other person for their honesty. A simple "Thanks for being upfront with me" shows maturity and leaves a positive impression, even if things didn't go as you hoped.

3. Avoid Overthinking It: After facing rejection, it's easy to replay the situation in your mind, wondering if you could have done something differently. But don't get stuck analyzing every detail. Instead, acknowledge that it didn't work out, accept that everyone faces rejection, and focus on moving forward.

4. Talk to Someone You Trust: If rejection leaves you feeling down, reach out to a friend, family member, or coach. Talking about it can help you process your emotions and remind you that you're not alone – everyone experiences rejection, even if they don't always show it.

5. Learn and Grow: Think of rejection as a stepping stone rather than a setback. Reflect on what you can learn from the experience, whether it's about improving communication skills, building confidence, or just understanding yourself better. Each experience helps you grow stronger and prepares you for the future.

Handling rejection with grace is about showing respect for yourself and others. By responding calmly, not taking it personally, and focusing on growth, you show strength and maturity. Remember, rejection is just a part of life's journey, not a final destination. How you handle it shapes who you become, so keep moving forward with confidence and respect.

EXAMPLE SCENARIOS:

- **Responding to Rejection:** You've been texting someone you really like, but they tell you they're not interested in dating right

now. Instead of getting upset, reply by saying "I appreciate your honesty. I hope we can still be friends." This shows maturity and respect for their feelings while keeping the door open for a friendship.
- **Not Getting a Desired Role:** You tried out for a spot on the school soccer team but didn't make the cut. Instead of sulking and going on about it, tell your friends "I'm bummed I didn't make it, but I'll keep practicing and try again next year!" This positive outlook demonstrates resilience and encourages you to keep pursuing your interests despite setbacks.

5. Dealing with Breakups: Moving Forward with Strength

Breakups can be tough, and it's normal to feel sad, confused, or even angry. Whether it was a short fling or a long-term relationship, ending things can bring up a mix of emotions. It's important to remember that it's okay to feel how you feel – healing takes time. Here are a few tips to help you move forward:

1. Allow Yourself to Grieve: Don't rush the healing process. It's okay to feel upset, frustrated, or even relieved. Let yourself feel, but don't let those feelings control your actions.

2. Talk to Someone You Trust: Whether it's a friend, family member, or even a counselor, talking things out can help clear your mind. They might offer support, perspective, or just a listening ear.

3. Keep Busy: Find things to do that you enjoy – play sports, hang out with friends, focus on hobbies. Staying busy helps you avoid obsessing over the breakup and lets you rediscover your interests.

4. Don't Rush into Another Relationship: Take time to heal before jumping into something new. It's important to understand what went wrong and learn from it so you can approach your next relationship with a fresh perspective.

5. Avoid Toxic Behaviors: It might feel tempting to stalk their social media or gossip about them, but that won't help you heal. Focus on positive actions that move you forward, not backward.

Remember, breakups are a part of life, and while they hurt, they also give you an opportunity to learn, grow, and become stronger.

Example Scenarios:

- **Talking to a Friend After a Breakup:** You've just gone through a breakup and feel all over the place. You text your friend Jake: "Hey, man, can we talk?" Over coffee, you share how you're feeling. Jake opens up about his own breakup, reminding you that it's okay to feel upset and that things will get better with time.
- **Staying Busy to Move On:** After the breakup, you feel low, so you decide to play basketball with your friends. This allows you to focus on the play instead of thinking about the breakup. By the end, you're laughing and enjoying yourself, realizing that staying active and hanging out with friends helps take your mind off the situation and lifts your mood.

6. Understanding Intimacy: Healthy Boundaries and Communication

Intimacy is more than just physical – it involves emotional connection, trust, and respect. It's important to understand that intimacy in a relationship should always be based on mutual respect and clear communication. Here's what to keep in mind:

1. Physical Boundaries: It's essential to have clear boundaries with your partner. Don't feel pressured to do anything you're not comfortable with. Respecting each other's limits shows maturity and ensures both people feel safe.

2. Emotional Intimacy: Emotional connection is just as important as physical intimacy. Share your thoughts, feelings, and experiences openly, but always respect your partner's privacy. Being vulnerable is part of creating a strong bond.

3. Communication is Key: Whether you're talking about your feelings, preferences, or concerns, open communication is critical. Be honest about what you want and listen to your partner's needs as well.

4. Consent is Essential: Always make sure both you and your partner are comfortable and consenting in any situation. Consent should be enthusiastic, ongoing, and respected at all times.

5. Pace Yourself: Don't rush into physical intimacy just to "fit in" or because you think you should. Take your time to understand each other and grow closer emotionally. A solid emotional connection makes any physical intimacy that much more meaningful.

Ultimately, intimacy is about trust and connection. By building a relationship based on respect, understanding, and clear communication, you'll create a healthy foundation for both emotional and physical closeness.

EXAMPLE SCENARIOS:

- **Talking About Boundaries with a Partner**: You and your partner are hanging out and things are getting more serious. You decide to ask, "Hey, I just want to make sure we're both comfortable with how things are going. Is there anything you would like to talk about?" This helps both of you feel respected and clear about what's okay and what's not.
- **Listening to Your Partner's Needs**: You're texting your partner and they mention they're feeling a little overwhelmed. Instead of brushing it off, you reply, "I hear you. What do you need right now? Do you want to talk, or should we do something fun to take your mind off things?" Listening and offering support shows that you care about her feelings and wants.

8. Managing Stress and Life's Challenges

Life can throw a lot at you, especially during your teenage years. This chapter focuses on understanding the common causes of teen stress and how to tackle them head-on. I'll explore effective coping strategies, from exercise to hobbies, that can help lighten your load. Building a support system is important, so I'll discuss how to surround yourself with people who lift you up. Finally, I'll emphasize the importance of asking for help when you need it. Let's equip you with the tools to handle life's challenges with confidence!

1. Understanding Common Causes of Teen Stress

Understanding what causes stress is a key part of learning to manage it. As a teenager, you're handling a lot – school, friendships, family expectations, and sometimes even a part-time job or sports practice.

These different areas of life can feel overwhelming, especially when it seems like everything is happening all at once. Let's take a closer look at some of the most common causes of stress for teens, along with ways to handle them.

1. Academic Pressure: Schoolwork, tests, and homework can pile up quickly, especially if you're trying to keep up good grades. The pressure to do well in school can feel intense, especially if you're balancing multiple classes and activities. When academics become stressful, consider creating a study schedule to break down tasks and take it one step at a time. Remember, it's okay to ask teachers for help or study with friends for extra support.

2. Social Situations: Friendships, dating, and fitting in are huge parts of teen life, but they can also be sources of stress. Feeling pressured to act or look a certain way, dealing with conflicts, or experiencing social anxiety are all normal but challenging. Try setting boundaries that feel right for you, and surround yourself with people who make you feel good about yourself. It's also okay to take breaks from social media, which can sometimes make things feel worse.

3. Family Expectations: Parents and family members often have hopes for you, whether it's about your grades, sports, or general behavior. Even when they mean well, this can sometimes feel like a lot to live up to. If family expectations are causing you stress, try having a calm conversation about what you're feeling. Let them know you're trying your best, and ask if they can help you find a balance.

4. Future Decisions: Thinking about the future – whether it's college, a job, or just what comes next – can be exciting but also overwhelming. If you're unsure about what you want, remember that it's okay to take things one step at a time. Talk to people you trust, like friends, family, or school counselors, who can offer guidance and perspective.

Recognizing these common causes of stress is the first step toward managing it. By understanding what's making you feel tense, you can start to develop strategies to handle each situation healthily. Stress is normal, but learning to deal with it will make you stronger and more prepared for life's challenges.

EXAMPLE SCENARIOS:

- **Academic Pressure:** You have a big exam coming up, and the stress is mounting. Instead of letting it overwhelm you, recognize that juggling homework, studying, and extracurricular activities is a lot. Break your study sessions into manageable chunks and talk to a teacher about any topics you're struggling with. This proactive approach will help ease your stress and set you up for success.
- **Social Expectations:** You feel anxious about fitting in with your friends, especially when they post about fun outings on social media. Instead of letting this pressure get to you, remind yourself that everyone has their own challenges and reach out to a close friend to go hang out one-on-one. This will foster deeper connections and reduce the stress of comparing yourself to others.

2. Coping Strategies: Exercise, Hobbies, and More

Managing stress effectively is all about finding what works for you. Exercise, hobbies, and other coping strategies can go a long way in helping you feel balanced and ready to take on challenges. Here are some practical ways to handle stress and boost your well-being:

1. Get Moving with Exercise: Exercise is one of the best ways to relieve stress. Physical activity, like running, biking, or even playing sports with friends, helps your body release endorphins – natural mood boosters that can lift your spirits and reduce anxiety. You don't have to hit the gym for hours; even a quick ten to fifteen minutes can make a difference. Find something active you enjoy, and try to make it a regular part of your week.

2. Dive into a Hobby: Hobbies are a great way to unwind and take a break from the things that stress you out. Whether it's painting, playing an instrument, writing, or working on a cool project, hobbies allow you to relax while doing something you enjoy. Think about what interests you or what you've always wanted to try – exploring new activities can be fun and keep your mind off stressors.

3. Practice Relaxation Techniques: Calming practices like deep breathing, meditation, or stretching can help when you're feeling overwhelmed. Just a few minutes spent focusing on your breath or stretching can clear your mind and make it easier to deal with stress. You can find guided meditation apps or YouTube videos to get started; these techniques might feel strange at first, but with practice, they can be incredibly helpful.

4. Set Realistic Goals: When you've got a lot on your plate, it's easy to feel overwhelmed. Breaking big tasks into smaller steps and setting achievable goals can make things feel more manageable. For example, if you have a big project, try dividing it into daily tasks. This way, you'll feel accomplished with each small step and stay motivated.

5. Stay Connected: Spending time with friends, family, or people you trust can help you feel supported. Talking through what's stressing you out can provide relief and remind you that you're not alone. Don't hesitate to reach out to those close to you – they can offer encouragement and advice.

6. Make Time for Fun and Relaxation: Taking breaks and having downtime is essential. Whether it's playing a game, reading, or just hanging out with friends, doing things you love gives you a chance to recharge and step away from stressful situations.

Trying different strategies will help you discover what works best for you. Building good habits now can make it easier to handle stress and keep yourself balanced for the future.

Example Scenarios:

- **Using Exercise as a Stress Reliever:** After a long week of exams and assignments, you feel overwhelmed and stressed. Instead of binge-watching your favorite show, go for a run. Put on your headphones and listen to your favorite playlist. As you run, you'll notice the tension in your shoulders easing and your mind clearing. You'll end your run feeling lighter and ready to tackle new challenges with a fresh perspective.
- **Engaging in Hobbies for Relaxation:** You've been feeling anxious about social situations and schoolwork. To cope, you pick up your guitar, something you love but haven't done in a while. As you play, you lose track of time and focus solely on the music.

Creative outlets like musical instruments help distract you from stress and give you a sense of accomplishment, reminding you that it's important to make time for the things you enjoy.

3. Building a Support System

Having a solid support system can make a big difference in how you handle stress and challenges, especially as you face new experiences and responsibilities. Whether it's dealing with school stress, friendship issues, or just feeling overwhelmed, having people to lean on helps keep you grounded. Here's how to start building your own support network:

1. Lean on Friends: Friends are often the first people we turn to, and for a good reason. They're there to listen, offer advice, or simply be with you during tough times. Try making friends with classmates or teammates, and spend time getting to know people who share your interests. Friendships take time, but investing in these connections can help you feel less alone when things get challenging.

2. Stay Connected with Family: Even if you're more independent now, family can still be an important source of support. They know you better than most people and often have valuable insights or advice. Keeping in touch, whether by phone, text, or face-to-face, can help you feel connected to home. Don't be afraid to open up about what's going on; your family will likely appreciate your honesty and want to help however they can.

3. Seek Guidance from Mentors or Counselors: School counselors or other mentors, like teachers or coaches, are great resources if you're going through a tough time. Talking to someone who is trained to listen can help you work through your feelings and find new ways to handle stress. Counseling is confidential, so you can express yourself freely without worry. Many students find that talking to a professional can help them gain a fresh perspective on their problems.

4. Put Yourself Out There: Building a support system means making an effort to connect. Join a club, try out for a sport, or just introduce yourself to people in your classes. Taking that first step can feel awkward, but the more you reach out, the easier it becomes to form meaningful connections.

5. Be Open About Your Needs: It's okay to let people know when you're struggling. If friends, family, or a counselor understand what you're going through, they can support you better. Being honest about your needs helps build trust and strengthens your support system.

A strong support network doesn't just happen overnight, but by reaching out, staying connected, and being open about your needs, you'll have people you can count on in good times and bad. Knowing there's a group of people who care about you can make life's challenges a little easier to handle.

Example Scenarios:

- **Reaching Out to Friends:** You've been feeling a bit isolated lately and noticed that school has become overwhelming. Instead of trying to deal with everything on your own, reach out to a couple of close friends by texting them "Hey, can we hang out this weekend? I could really use some company." When you meet up, share what's been on your mind. Just talking about it will help lighten your load, and you'll realize your friends are there to support you, too.
- **Connecting with a Trusted Adult:** You're facing some challenges in school, and the pressure is starting to build. Instead of keeping it all bottled up, go talk to your favorite teacher. After class, ask them "Can I share some stuff that's been stressing me out?" Your teacher will appreciate this gesture and give you practical advice, showing you that it's okay to seek help and that adults can be valuable allies in your journey.

4. Asking for Help When Things Get Tough

Asking for help can feel intimidating, but it's a powerful way to manage stress and keep yourself on track when things get tough. Recognizing when you need a hand shows maturity and self-awareness, not weakness. There will be times when things pile up, whether it's school pressures, relationship challenges, or just feeling overwhelmed. Here's how you can get support when you need it:

1. Reach Out to Trusted Adults: Parents, teachers, or school counselors are there to help. If you're feeling stressed, sad, or lost, don't hesitate to talk to an adult you trust. They've likely been through similar experiences and can offer advice, encouragement, or simply a listening ear. Even if you're not sure what to say, just starting the conversation can be a huge relief.

2. Use Peer Support: Sometimes it helps to talk to someone your age who "gets it." Many schools have peer support groups or even student-led activities where you can connect with others facing similar challenges. Sharing with a friend or classmate who understands what you're going through can be comforting. You may find you're not alone in your struggles, and together, you can find solutions or just share some laughs to lighten the load.

3. Explore School Resources: Most schools offer resources like counseling or wellness workshops focused on handling stress, building healthy habits, and staying balanced. School counselors are trained to listen without judgment and provide helpful strategies for managing emotions. Don't be afraid to set up an appointment or attend a workshop; these services are meant to support you.

4. Be Open About What You Need: Whether it's extra support with schoolwork, time to recharge, or just someone to listen, let people know what would help you most. Maybe you need advice on a specific problem or simply a distraction from stress. Expressing what you need doesn't make you a burden – instead, it helps others understand how they can best support you.

Asking for help is a sign of strength, not a flaw. By reaching out to others, you're showing you care about your own well-being. When things get challenging, remember that support is there if you're willing to take that first step and ask.

EXAMPLE SCENARIOS:

- **Reaching Out to a Classmate:** You've been struggling with a difficult math concept and feel stuck. Instead of trying to figure it out alone, try asking a classmate who seems to grasp it well. Say "Hey, I'm having a tough time with this topic. Could you help me understand it better?" Your classmate is happy to assist and even offers to study together before the next test. Doing this will not only help you learn but also strengthen your friendship.
- **Talking to a Parent:** After a tough week at school, you feel overwhelmed and anxious. Instead of hiding your feelings, sit down with your parents and say "I've had a rough time lately, and I could really use someone to talk to." Your parents listen and encourage you to share what's bothering you. Having these conversations will help you feel lighter and will remind you that it's okay to lean on family when times are tough.

9. Emotional Intelligence and Mental Health

Understanding your emotions and how to manage them is key to navigating life's ups and downs. In this chapter, I'll delve into emotional intelligence, exploring techniques for managing anger and coping with feelings of sadness, grief, or loss. You'll learn about mindfulness practices that help regulate your emotions and keep you grounded. I'll also go over how to recognize when it's time to seek support from others. By building your emotional toolkit, you'll be better prepared to handle whatever life throws your way.

1. Anger Management Basics

Anger is a powerful emotion, and during your teenage years, it can sometimes feel hard to control. But learning how to manage anger can help you handle tough situations calmly, improve your relationships, and maintain your mental well-being. Anger is natural, but the way you deal with it makes a big difference. Here are some basics to help you recognize and control anger when it arises:

1. Identify Your Triggers: Start by figuring out what usually sets off your anger. Maybe it's a tough day at school, disagreements with friends, or feeling misunderstood by family. Try keeping a journal to track moments when you feel angry and note what triggered those feelings. This can help you recognize patterns and prepare to handle similar situations calmly in the future.

2. Find Healthy Outlets: Physical activities are great ways to let off steam. Exercise, sports, or even going for a walk can help release built-up anger and improve your mood. If you're more creative, try expressing yourself through writing, drawing, or playing music. These outlets not only calm you down but help you make something positive out of your anger.

3. Practice Relaxation Techniques: Learning techniques like deep breathing, meditation, or progressive muscle relaxation can help calm you down in heated moments. When you feel your anger rising, take a few deep breaths or count to ten. These simple actions can help you think more clearly and respond in a more controlled way.

4. Use 'I' Statements: When talking about what's bothering you, try using "I" statements to explain your feelings without blaming others. For example, instead of saying "You never listen to me," try "I feel frustrated when my opinions aren't considered." This helps people understand your perspective without feeling attacked.

5. Take a Timeout: If you feel your anger escalating, step away from the situation. Taking a break gives you a chance to cool down and consider how to respond more thoughtfully. Sometimes, just a few minutes of quiet can help prevent things from getting worse.

6. Work to Resolve Conflicts: Don't let anger linger. When you're ready, approach the situation with the goal of finding a solution. Resolving conflicts can keep anger from building up and help you handle similar issues better in the future.

7. Communicate Openly: Once you're calm, talk about your feelings. Explain why you felt angry and listen to the other person's perspective. This approach can improve understanding and prevent misunderstandings from happening again.

Learning these basics can help you control your anger rather than letting it control you. With practice, you'll find it easier to handle even the most challenging moments calmly and confidently.

Example Scenarios:

- **Taking a Break After an Argument:** You just had a heated argument with a friend over a group project, and you're feeling really angry. Instead of saying something you might regret, go take a walk around the school to cool off. As you walk, focus on your breathing and try to let go of the frustration. After a bit of time, you'll feel calmer and you'll be able to approach your friend to discuss the disagreement more calmly and respectfully.
- **Handling Frustration During Practice:** During soccer practice, you miss a shot you've been working hard to perfect, and you feel

anger bubbling up. Rather than kicking the ball away or taking it out on teammates, step aside, pause and take a few deep breaths to reset. By managing your frustration, you'll be better able to focus on the next drill, staying positive and engaged for the rest of the practice.

2. Handling Sadness, Grief, and Loss

Sadness, grief, and loss are difficult feelings, but learning to handle them can help you build emotional resilience (the ability to bounce back from difficult or stressful situations). Whether it's losing a loved one, ending a friendship, or facing a big change, everyone experiences grief differently. Understanding what you're going through and having tools to cope can help you heal over time. Here's a closer look at grief and some ways to manage it.

UNDERSTANDING GRIEF

Grief isn't a straight line; it often comes in stages. You might go through some or all of these stages, and they don't always happen in order:

1. Denial – At first, it might feel unreal, as if the loss didn't happen. This is a natural reaction to overwhelming emotions.

2. Anger – It's normal to feel angry, sometimes at the situation or even at yourself or others.

3. Bargaining – You might start thinking "what if" and wonder if things could've gone differently.

4. Depression – Feelings of sadness and loss can be heavy during this stage.

5. Acceptance – With time, you may start to come to terms with what happened.

Knowing that these feelings are normal can help you feel less overwhelmed by your emotions.

COPING STRATEGIES FOR GRIEF

1. Allow Yourself to Feel: Don't ignore your feelings. Let yourself feel the sadness, anger, or frustration without judgment. Trying to suppress emotions often makes them harder to handle later.

2. Talk About It: Find someone you trust, like a friend, family member, or counselor, to share your feelings. Talking can make the grief feel lighter.

3. Maintain Routines: Keeping a routine can bring stability during tough times. Even small things, like having breakfast or going for a walk, can help you feel grounded.

4. Take Care of Your Physical Health: Your body and mind are connected. Make sure you get enough sleep, eat well, and stay active. Physical health can support your emotional healing.

5. Seek Professional Help if Needed: If grief feels too heavy, talking to a counselor can offer support. They can guide you through this difficult time.

FINDING MEANING IN LOSS

Engaging in activities that help you remember what you've lost can bring comfort.

- **Honor Their Memory**: You could create a scrapbook, participate in a charity event, or simply write down memories.
- **Find Creative Outlets**: Try expressing yourself through art, writing, or music. Creativity can be a powerful way to release your feelings.

Grieving is personal, and there's no set time for "moving on." Take things at your own pace. In time, you might find the strength and resilience that will help you grow, while still cherishing the memories you hold close. Grieving is tough, but with patience and support, you'll find healing.

EXAMPLE SCENARIOS:

- **Dealing with Disappointment After Losing a Game:** Your team lost an important game you'd been training hard for, and you feel a deep sadness and disappointment. Instead of bottling it up, take some time to reflect on what went well and what you can improve. Later, talk to a friend or family member about how you're feeling; this will help you process the loss. Sharing your feelings and getting support reminds you that setbacks happen and that you can bounce back stronger.
- **Coping with Grief After a Family Pet Passes Away:** You recently lost a family pet, and the sadness feels overwhelming. Instead of pushing the feelings away, allow yourself to feel sad and even cry when you need to. Pour your feelings into creating a small memory scrapbook with pictures and notes about favorite moments with your pet. This will help you focus on the good memories, and over time, you'll find comfort in remembering the happy times you shared together.

3. Mindfulness and Emotional Regulation

Learning to manage emotions can feel like a superpower, especially during the teenage years when emotions can feel intense and hard to control. One of the best tools to help with this is mindfulness, which is the practice of paying close attention to the present moment without judgment. Being mindful helps you understand your emotions better and gives you tools to respond to them calmly and thoughtfully, instead of letting them control you. Here's how mindfulness and emotional regulation can make life easier – and some tips to get you started.

WHY MINDFULNESS MATTERS FOR EMOTIONAL REGULATION

When you're feeling overwhelmed, it's easy to let emotions take over. This can lead to saying or doing things you might regret, especially when you're angry, stressed, or frustrated. Mindfulness teaches you to recognize these feelings as they happen, so you can respond in a way that feels more in control. Practicing mindfulness can make it easier to stay calm, make better decisions, and even improve your relationships with friends and family.

How to Practice Mindfulness and Control Emotions

Here are some simple, practical techniques to start working mindfulness into your life:

1. Pause and Breathe: When you feel a strong emotion coming on, try taking a few deep breaths. Count to four as you breathe in, and count to four as you breathe out. This simple act can slow down your heart rate and give you a moment to think before reacting.

2. Observe Your Emotions: Try to notice what emotions you're feeling without judgment. Are you angry, sad, frustrated, or anxious? Just label the feeling in your mind. Instead of thinking "I *am* angry," think "I *feel* angry." This small shift helps remind you that emotions are temporary; they come and go.

3. Body Scans: A quick body scan can help you relax. Close your eyes and mentally "scan" your body from head to toe. Notice if you're holding tension anywhere (like clenched fists or a tight jaw) and try to release it. This simple practice helps you connect with your body and reduce stress.

4. Use Visualization: When an emotion feels too intense, visualize it as a wave coming and going, or imagine placing it in a box you can set aside. This can help you feel more control over it and reduce its power over your actions.

5. Practice Daily: Mindfulness works best when practiced regularly. Try setting aside a few minutes each day to sit quietly, focus on your breathing, and let go of thoughts. Apps or guided videos can help if you're just starting out.

Building Emotional Awareness

Becoming more aware of your emotions helps you understand them and allows you to respond thoughtfully. It takes practice, but over time, mindfulness can help you feel calmer and more resilient when dealing with challenges. Emotions are a big part of life, but with mindfulness, you can learn to handle them in a way that helps you stay in control. The more you practice, the stronger and more self-aware you become – just like any other skill.

EXAMPLE SCENARIOS:

- **Using Breathing Exercises Before a Big Presentation:** You're about to give a class presentation, and you can feel your heart racing with nerves. Instead of letting the stress build up, take a few minutes to do a simple breathing exercise. Close your eyes, breathe in deeply for four counts, hold it, and then exhale for four counts. This will help calm your nerves, steady your thoughts, and let you focus on the presentation, giving you a better sense of control and confidence.
- **Practicing Mindfulness to Manage Frustration:** You're working on a tricky homework assignment, and after struggling with a few problems, you start feeling frustrated and tempted to quit. Instead of giving up, pause, close your eyes, and take a few deep breaths to clear your mind. Then focus on one problem at a time instead of the whole assignment, reminding yourself that it's okay to take things slow. This mindful approach will help ease your frustration and let you finish with a clearer, more focused mind.

4. Recognizing When to Seek Support

Learning to recognize when it's time to seek support is an essential skill that shows strength, not weakness. Everyone faces difficult moments, and knowing when to reach out can make handling life's challenges easier and healthier. It's natural to want to deal with things on your own, but sometimes problems become too big or feel overwhelming. Recognizing this is a sign of maturity and emotional intelligence – and getting support can make a huge difference in finding solutions and feeling better.

How Do You Know When It's Time to Seek Help?

There are a few signs that may indicate it's time to reach out:

1. You're Feeling Overwhelmed: If you're constantly feeling stressed, worried, or weighed down, it might be a sign that you need support. When you feel overwhelmed, it's harder to think clearly, make good decisions, and feel like yourself.

2. It's Hard to Focus or Stay Motivated: Struggling to stay motivated in school, with friends, or in activities you usually enjoy could mean you're dealing with something bigger emotionally. This could be a sign that it's time to talk to someone.

3. Emotions Feel Uncontrollable: If you're having intense emotions like anger, sadness, or frustration that don't seem to go away or feel too powerful to handle, support can help. Everyone feels strong emotions, but if they're taking over, speaking up is the first step to feeling better.

4. You're Avoiding People or Activities: Not wanting to be around others or losing interest in activities can be a sign that you're dealing with something that needs attention. Talking to someone can help you understand and manage what's going on.

Where to Find Support

Once you've recognized you need help, here are some people or places to turn to:

1. Friends and Family: Talking to someone you trust, like a friend, sibling, or parent, can provide comfort and advice. Even just sharing what's on your mind can help you feel less alone.

2. School Counselors: Counselors are trained to help with issues like stress, relationships, and tough emotions. They're there to listen and support you without judgment.

3. Hotlines or Online Chats: If talking in person feels difficult, there are hotlines or online chat services like BetterHelp or Safe Helpline where you can connect with someone who can help.

Seeking help when you need it is a smart and positive choice. It doesn't mean you're giving up; it means you're building strength. Whether it's advice, a listening ear, or professional support, reaching out can make all the difference in handling life's challenges.

EXAMPLE SCENARIOS:

- **Reaching Out When School Feels Overwhelming:** You've noticed that your workload is piling up, and it's getting harder to keep up with assignments and test prep. You start feeling constantly stressed, even outside of school hours, and it's affecting your sleep. Realizing it's too much to handle alone, you decide to talk to a teacher or school counselor. They help you make a plan to manage your time better and suggest resources for extra help, which takes some of the pressure off and makes school feel more manageable.
- **Seeking Support for Difficult Emotions:** After a recent argument with a close friend, you've been feeling unusually down and can't shake a sense of sadness. Days pass, and it's still weighing on you, impacting your mood and energy. You decide to confide in a trusted family member or friend who listens, understands what you're going through, and provides advice on how to approach your friend. Sharing your feelings helps you feel less alone, and allows you to work through your emotions in a healthy way.

10. Technology and Social Media Use

In today's digital world, technology and social media play a huge role in our lives, shaping how we connect with friends and express ourselves, especially during our teenage years. In this chapter, I'll go over how to navigate these tools wisely, starting with setting healthy boundaries for screen time. You'll learn important strategies for staying safe online, practicing good digital etiquette, and protecting your personal information. By understanding these key aspects of technology use, you'll be equipped to make smart choices that enhance your online experiences without compromising your well-being.

1. Setting Boundaries with Screen Time

Balancing screen time with the need for rest is crucial, especially as screen use has become a big part of everyday life. Too much screen time, especially at night, can interfere with sleep, mood, and energy levels. Good sleep is essential for staying alert, focused, and in a positive mindset. However, the blue light from screens can disrupt the production of melatonin – a hormone that signals our bodies to sleep – making it harder to wind down and get restful sleep. Constant notifications and the urge to scroll can also keep your brain overstimulated when it should be relaxing.

Here are some simple tips to help set healthier boundaries between screen time and sleep:

1. Create a "Screen-Free" Bedtime Routine: Try to set aside your devices at least thirty to sixty minutes before going to sleep. Use this time to do something calming, like reading, journaling, or listening to music. A screen-free routine tells your brain it's time to wind down, making it easier to fall asleep.

2. Stick to a Sleep Schedule: Aim to go to bed and wake up at the same time every day, even on weekends. A regular sleep schedule keeps your body's internal clock steady, which helps you fall asleep and wake up feeling refreshed. This routine also helps reduce the chances of late-night scrolling.

3. Use Night Mode or Blue Light Filters: If you need to use your phone or laptop at night, turn on night mode or a blue light filter. These settings reduce the amount of blue light your screen emits, which can lessen the impact on your sleep. Still, it's best to limit screen time altogether close to bedtime.

4. Turn Off Notifications: Constant notifications can pull your attention back to your device, even if you're trying to wind down. Switch off notifications for non-essential apps in the evening or activate "Do Not Disturb" mode during bedtime hours.

5. Keep Devices Out of Reach: Try charging your phone or laptop away from your bed. This reduces the temptation to check it right before sleeping or if you wake up during the night.

Setting these boundaries helps protect your sleep and supports your mental health. A good night's rest boosts your mood, reduces stress, and sharpens your focus, making it easier to tackle daily challenges. Remember, finding balance is key – use your devices wisely, but make sure they don't get in the way of the rest your body and mind need to thrive.

Example Scenarios:

- **Taking Breaks During Homework:** You're studying for a big test, but your phone keeps buzzing with notifications. Instead of checking every message, set a timer for thirty minutes of focused study and leave your phone in another room. After the timer goes off, give yourself a five-minute break to check messages before going back to study mode. This way, you'll stay productive without getting sucked into screen time.
- **Setting a Screen-Free Time at Night:** You've noticed that scrolling through social media before bed makes it harder to fall asleep. To help, put your phone away an hour before bed and spend the time reading or doing something relaxing instead. Over time, this habit will help you feel more rested and alert during the day, making it easier to concentrate in school and enjoy your day.

2. Staying Safe on Social Media

Social media is a huge part of our lives – it's where we connect with friends, share moments, and even learn new things. But being on social media also means being smart about safety. Staying safe doesn't just mean protecting your information but also keeping your confidence and mental health in check. Social media can make it easy to feel like everyone else's life is perfect, which might leave you feeling down. Understanding how to handle these platforms wisely can help you enjoy them without getting caught up in negativity or risky situations.

Here are some simple strategies for staying safe and confident on social media:

1. Set Time Limits: Spending too much time online can make it easy to get caught in comparison traps, which can mess with your self-esteem. The American Academy of Pediatrics suggests keeping screen time to one or two hours a day for entertainment. Use built-in screen time tools to keep track, and make sure you're still focusing on friends, family, and things you love offline.

2. Remember It's Just a Highlight Reel: People mostly post their best moments online – not their struggles. Keeping this in mind can prevent you from comparing your real life to someone's polished profile. Everyone has ups and downs, even if it doesn't seem that way on their social media.

3. Use Privacy Settings: Protect your privacy by controlling who can see your posts and personal info. Check your settings to make sure only friends or approved followers can see your content. This helps you avoid unwanted attention or potential issues with people you don't know.

4. Engage Positively: Try to spread positivity and encouragement rather than getting involved in negative interactions. Avoid arguments or harsh comments that could lead to unnecessary stress or conflict. Supporting others makes social media a healthier space for everyone.

5. Stay Informed and Aware: New social media trends pop up all the time, and some of them come with risks. Stay updated on privacy tips and safety tools, and share what you learn with friends and family so they can stay safe, too.

6. Project Your Privacy Online: Be mindful of what you share on social media. Avoid posting sensitive information like your address, phone number, or email address to protect your privacy and prevent potential risks like identity theft or unwanted attention.

By following these steps, you can enjoy social media in a way that's fun and safe, without letting it impact your mental well-being. Remember, social media is just a part of life – not the whole picture. Being mindful of how it makes you feel and setting smart boundaries can help you get the best out of it.

EXAMPLE SCENARIOS:

- **Thinking Before You Post:** You're excited to share a photo from your day out with friends, but before posting, double-check the background to make sure there's nothing personal, like school logos or street names, that could reveal your location. This simple habit

keeps your private details off the Internet and helps you control who knows where you've been.
- **Handling a Message from a Stranger:** You get a friend request from someone you don't know. Instead of accepting, check if you have any mutual friends and review their profile. Since they seem unfamiliar, ignore the request and adjust your privacy settings to make sure only friends can see your posts. By doing so, you'll keep your social circle safe and avoid any unwanted contact.

3. Digital Etiquette: The Do's and Don'ts

Navigating social media, texts, and online chats can be tricky. Knowing the basics of "digital etiquette" (also called "netiquette") can help you avoid misunderstandings, show respect, and communicate confidently. Good digital etiquette means thinking about how your words and actions online affect others, which can build trust and make your online interactions more positive. Here are some basic do's and don'ts to help you stay respectful and thoughtful in the digital world.

THE DO'S:

1. Think Before You Post: Once something is posted online, you can't take it down. Consider whether a photo, comment, or video is something you'd be comfortable with everyone seeing – not just now but also in the future. Ask yourself "Would I say or show this face-to-face?"

2. Be Respectful: Treat others online the way you'd like to be treated. Avoid making rude or harsh comments, even if you disagree with someone. Respectful responses can keep conversations constructive, whether you're chatting with friends or in a group setting.

3. Use Emojis and Tone Wisely: Text can be hard to interpret without the visual cues of real-life conversation. Adding emojis can help convey tone, like whether you're being playful or serious. Just don't overuse them; a well-placed emoji can help clarify a message without being confusing.

4. Give Credit: If you share someone else's work, whether it's a photo, video, meme, or quote, make sure to give them credit. Tagging or mentioning them shows respect and avoids any appearance of stealing.

THE DON'TS:

1. Don't Overshare Personal Information: Things like your address, phone number, or school should be kept private. Oversharing can lead to safety risks or unwanted attention. Remember that even close friends can have accounts that aren't totally secure.

2. Avoid Public Arguments: Online arguments are rarely productive, and they can quickly get out of control. If you have an issue with someone, try handling it privately through a direct message or even talking face-to-face.

3. Don't Spam: Reposting or sharing something multiple times in a short period can be annoying for others. Respect people's timelines and inboxes by sharing once or twice and allowing others to engage if they're interested.

4. Watch Out for Cyberbullying: Refrain from any behavior that could be hurtful, even if it's meant as a joke. Avoid tagging people in unflattering photos, sharing memes at someone's expense, or posting sarcastic comments. If you see someone else being bullied online, show support for them or report the behavior.

Understanding digital etiquette is about creating a space where everyone feels respected and valued. By practicing these tips, you can build a good online reputation and contribute positively to your social media and digital communities. Remember, the way you act online reflects on you, so make sure it's something you'd be proud of.

EXAMPLE SCENARIOS:

- **Pausing Before You Reply:** You receive a message that feels a bit rude from a friend who didn't respond to your text right away. Instead of firing off an angry reply, take a deep breath and

consider that they might be busy. Later, they explained they were just having a rough day. By staying calm, you avoided a misunderstanding and kept things friendly.
- **Group Chat Awareness:** In a group chat, a friend shares something that seems personal. You notice that another friend responds with a joke that feels a bit insensitive. Instead of jumping in or ignoring it, gently steer the conversation back on track with a supportive comment. Your response shows respect and helps keep the group chat a positive place for everyone.

4. Protecting Personal Information

In today's digital world, protecting your personal information is essential. Whether you're scrolling through social media, chatting with friends, or playing games online, knowing what to keep private can help you stay safe and prevent unwanted risks. Hackers, scammers, and even some apps can take advantage of personal information, so it's important to be mindful of what you share and how you share it. Here are a few simple steps to keep your information safe online.

1. Limit What You Share: Think carefully before posting personal details, such as your full name, address, phone number, or school name, especially on public profiles. These details can reveal more about you than you may realize. Even seemingly harmless information like your birthdate can be pieced together to guess passwords or answer security questions.

2. Adjust Your Privacy Settings: Most social media platforms and apps have privacy settings that let you control who can see your posts, photos, and personal details. Set your accounts to private and review your settings regularly, as updates can sometimes reset them. Limit the visibility of your information to friends and people you know personally rather than "Friends of Friends" or "Public."

3. Be Cautious About Location Sharing: While sharing your location with close friends can be convenient, it's generally safer to turn off location sharing on social media posts. Some platforms automatically add location tags, so check before you post. By disabling these features, you're less likely to have your whereabouts tracked by strangers.

4. Use Strong, Unique Passwords: Having a strong, unique password for each account makes it harder for hackers to access your information. Avoid easy-to-guess passwords like "password123" or "letmein," and include a mix of letters, numbers, and symbols. Consider using a password manager to keep track of your passwords safely.

5. Think Before You Click: Be wary of links or attachments from unknown sources, as they can contain malware designed to steal your information. Phishing scams, where someone pretends to be a trusted contact to trick you into giving out personal info, are also common. Double-check links and don't hesitate to delete anything suspicious.

6. Avoid Using Public Wi-Fi for Sensitive Tasks: If you need to access your accounts, shop online, or check personal information, it's best to avoid public Wi-Fi, which is often unsecured. Instead, wait until you're on a trusted network, or use a virtual private network (VPN) to keep your data safe.

By protecting your personal information, you're taking control of your privacy and staying secure online. Remember, a few careful steps today can help you avoid issues in the future, giving you more freedom and peace of mind in your digital life.

EXAMPLE SCENARIOS:

- **Being Cautious with Apps:** You're about to download a new game on your phone, but the app requests access to your location, contacts, and camera – things the game doesn't really need. Instead of just clicking "Accept," you decide not to download it until you can check reviews to see if the app is trustworthy. By thinking twice, you protect your personal info from unnecessary access.
- **Keeping Passwords Private:** A friend asks for the password to your streaming service account. Instead of sharing it, you let them know you'd rather keep your passwords private. You can offer to watch something together, but by politely saying no, you're keeping your accounts secure.

11. Driving and Car Ownership Basics

Getting your driver's license is an exciting milestone that opens up a whole new world of independence and responsibility. In this chapter, I'll cover the essential skills and knowledge you need to navigate the roads safely and confidently. From understanding basic driving tips to mastering car maintenance and managing the costs of ownership, you'll learn how to take care of your vehicle and yourself on the road. By the end of this chapter, you'll be ready to drive with confidence and make smart choices about car ownership.

1. Getting a License and Basic Driving Tips

Getting your driver's license is a major milestone! It brings freedom but also new responsibilities, and understanding the basics can make the process easier and help you be a safe driver. Here's a breakdown of how to get your license and some essential tips to start your driving journey off right.

1. Start with a Learner's Permit: Most places require new drivers to start with a learner's permit. To get one, you'll usually need to pass a written test covering road signs, traffic laws, and safety rules. Once you have your permit, you can start driving, but only with a licensed adult in the passenger seat. This period helps you gain experience on the road with someone who can guide you.

2. Practice with Supervised Driving Hours: To qualify for a full or provisional license, you'll often need to complete a certain number of supervised driving hours. These hours are meant to prepare you for various road situations, like driving at night, in the rain, or during busy traffic. Practicing with an experienced driver helps you build confidence and master essential skills before driving on your own.

3. Get Your Provisional or Intermediate License: Once you've met the practice requirements and reached the minimum age (usually around sixteen or seventeen), you can apply for a provisional or intermediate license. This stage often comes with restrictions, like driving curfews or limits on how many passengers you can have. This intermediate phase helps you ease into driving solo with fewer distractions and reduced risks.

4. Prepare for the Road Test: To get your full license, you'll need to pass a road test, where an examiner observes your driving skills. They'll watch for your ability to follow road rules, make safe turns, park, and drive responsibly. Practicing these skills ahead of time can help you feel prepared and relaxed on test day.

Basic Driving Tips for New Drivers

Learning the fundamentals of safe driving will help you navigate the roads with confidence and responsibility. Here are a few key tips:

- **Always Buckle Up**: It's the law, and it's your first line of defense in an accident.

- **Stay Focused**: Avoid distractions, like using your phone or adjusting the radio, which can take your attention off the road.
- **Follow Speed Limits**: Speeding reduces your reaction time and increases accident risk, so stick to posted limits.
- **Keep a Safe Distance**: Leave enough space between you and the car in front of you to avoid sudden stops or collisions. Use the three-second rule by picking a fixed point on the road; if you reach it before counting to three after the car in front passes it, increase your distance. In poor weather or at higher speeds, consider extending this to four or five seconds for extra safety.
- **Know How to Handle Emergencies**: If you feel uncertain or unsafe, pull over when it's safe, turn on your hazard lights, and ask for help if needed.

Getting your license is about more than just driving – it's about responsibility and making smart choices. By following these steps and tips, you'll be prepared for a safe and enjoyable driving experience.

Example Scenarios:

- **Practicing Before the Test:** You've been preparing for your driving test, and your dad offers to take you to an empty parking lot for some practice. Focus on parallel parking and making smooth turns, paying attention to small details like using your turn signals. This kind of practice will make you feel more confident and in control, which will pay off on test day.
- **Handling Minor Road Distractions:** On one of your early solo drives, you're at an intersection when you hear a loud siren. Instead of panicking, take a quick look around, spot the ambulance, and wait until it passes before safely proceeding. Staying calm and alert in these moments shows you're able to handle distractions and keep your focus on the road.

2. Car Maintenance 101: Oil, Tires, and More

Taking care of your car is easier than it sounds, and it can make a big difference in how well it runs and how safe it is. By doing regular maintenance like oil changes and tire care, you'll keep your car in top shape and avoid surprise breakdowns. Here's a quick rundown of some basic maintenance tasks and tips to help you get started.

1. Follow a Routine Maintenance Schedule: Cars need regular check-ups just like we do! Routine maintenance helps catch small problems early before they turn into big, expensive ones. Most cars benefit from a check-up every 5,000 to 7,500 miles (8,000 to 12,000 kilometers) or about every six months. Routine maintenance can keep your car running smoothly, improve fuel efficiency, and help your car last longer.

2. Regular Oil Changes: Oil is the lifeblood of your car's engine, keeping all the parts moving smoothly. Most cars need an oil change every 5,000 to 7,500 miles (8,000 to 12,000 kilometers), but check your owner's manual for specifics. Use the oil type recommended by the manufacturer for the best results, and remember to change the oil filter too, as it keeps your oil clean by trapping dirt and debris. Sticking to regular oil changes is one of the easiest ways to keep your engine healthy.

3. Tire Rotations, Alignments, and Balancing: Tires wear out unevenly, especially the front and back tires. Rotating them every 5,000 to 7,500 miles (8,000 to 12,000 kilometers) helps them wear evenly and last longer. Tire alignment, which adjusts the angles of your wheels, is important too; it keeps your car stable and improves handling. Regular alignment checks keep your car driving straight and prevent uneven tire wear. Balancing your tires makes sure they're evenly weighted, giving you a smoother ride and avoiding wear and tear on your suspension.

4. Check Tire Pressure Regularly: Properly inflated tires are safer and help your car get better gas mileage. Too much or too little air can lead to blowouts or uneven tire wear. Use a tire gauge to check your tire pressure every month, especially as temperatures change, and keep it within the range recommended by the manufacturer (usually found on a sticker inside the driver's door or in your owner's manual).

5. Choosing the Right Fuel: Using the right fuel is essential for good engine performance. Most cars run perfectly on regular unleaded gas, while others need premium. Putting in the wrong fuel can affect performance and could harm the engine over time. Just follow the manufacturer's recommendation, usually found in your owner's manual or inside the gas cap.

6. Get to Know Your Owner's Manual: Your car's manual has all the answers! It tells you when to get oil changes, what type of oil to use, how to check fluid levels, and more. Spending a few minutes with it can make a huge difference in keeping your car running smoothly.

By sticking to these simple car care routines, you'll keep your car running better, save money, and help prevent breakdowns. Plus, taking good care of your car is a big step toward being a responsible driver.

Example Scenarios:

- **Checking the Oil:** After a long weekend road trip, you notice your car seems to be running a little differently, so you decide to check the oil level. Following a quick YouTube tutorial, you pop the

hood, pull out the dipstick, and find the level is low. You add a quart of oil from the garage, feeling more confident about checking the oil regularly to keep your engine running smoothly.
- **Inspecting Tire Pressure:** One cold morning, you notice a dashboard light for low tire pressure. Instead of ignoring it, you head to a nearby gas station and check each tire's pressure. You realize one tire is slightly below the recommended level, so you add air until it's balanced. This small habit will keep your car's tires in good shape, improve gas mileage, and keep you safer on the road.

3. Safe Driving Practices

Driving safely is about more than just following the rules; it's about keeping yourself and others safe on the road. Here are some important practices that can help you become a responsible and defensive driver.

Defensive Driving

Defensive driving means staying alert to potential dangers and being ready to respond quickly. It's not about driving slowly but about driving wisely. Here are a few tips:

- **Anticipate Hazards**: Keep an eye on the road and be aware of other drivers, pedestrians, and potential hazards like changing road conditions.
- **Keep a Safe Distance**: Follow the "three-second rule" by ensuring there's a three-second gap between you and the car ahead. This gives you enough time to react if the other driver suddenly stops.
- **Avoid Distractions**: Keep your eyes on the road. Texting, eating, or using in-car gadgets can wait until you're safely parked.

Consider Taking a Defensive Driving Course

Defensive driving courses teach advanced driving skills that can increase your safety and confidence on the road. Plus, some insurance companies offer discounts for completing a certified course. Check with your local DMV (Department of Motor Vehicles) or a trusted driving school to find classes in your area or online.

Traffic Laws and Regulations

Following traffic laws keeps you and others safe. Here are a few essentials to remember:

- **Observe Speed Limits**: Speed limits are there for a reason and vary by area, such as school zones, residential streets, or highways. Follow them, and adjust your speed based on weather or road conditions.
- **Understand Right of Way**: Knowing who goes first at intersections, pedestrian crossings, and roundabouts helps prevent confusion and accidents. Yield to pedestrians and always use your turn signals to let other drivers know your intentions.
- **Watch for Penalties**: Breaking traffic laws can lead to fines or points on your record. Too many points can even lead to license suspension or increased insurance rates. Reckless driving, like speeding or driving under the influence, has serious consequences, including fines and possibly a criminal record.

Emergency Preparedness

Being prepared for emergencies on the road is key to staying safe:

- **Have a Car Emergency Kit**: Stock a kit with essentials like a first-aid kit, flashlight, tire inflator, jumper cables, and basic tools.
- **Know What to Do in a Breakdown**: If your car breaks down, move it to a safe spot if possible. Turn on your hazard lights to alert other drivers, and call for roadside assistance. Keep track of your location using nearby landmarks or intersections for quicker help.
- **Handling Accidents**: If you're in an accident, stay calm. Check for injuries, turn on hazard lights, and move to a safe spot if

possible. Exchange contact and insurance information with the other driver, take photos of the scene, and report the incident to local authorities to get an official record.

By practicing these safe driving tips, you'll develop good habits that not only protect you but also make you a courteous, responsible driver.

EXAMPLE SCENARIOS:

- **Keeping a Safe Following Distance:** While driving to school in a bit of rain, you notice the car in front of you braking unexpectedly. Thankfully, you remembered to keep a good following distance. You're able to stop safely without any close calls, reinforcing how important it is to maintain space, especially in wet conditions.
- **Avoiding Phone Distractions:** You're on your way to meet friends when a text notification pops up. Instead of checking it, you remember to stay focused on the road. At a stoplight, you quickly turn on "Do Not Disturb" mode. When you arrive, your friends are impressed that you prioritized safety over distractions.

4. Managing Car Costs: Gas, Insurance, and Maintenance

Owning a car involves more than just driving it; there are also ongoing costs to manage, like gas, insurance, and maintenance. Learning how to handle these expenses wisely will help you keep your car running well without emptying your wallet.

GAS COSTS

Fuel is one of the biggest ongoing expenses for car owners. Here are some ways to stretch your gas budget:

- **Drive Smoothly**: Avoid rapid acceleration and heavy braking, as

these can burn through fuel quickly. Instead, try to drive at a steady pace whenever possible.
- **Plan Your Trips**: Combine errands into one trip to reduce mileage and save on gas. You'll save both time and money by not having to make multiple trips.
- **Check Tire Pressure**: Keeping your tires properly inflated helps improve fuel efficiency. Underinflated tires cause your engine to work harder, which uses more fuel.

Understanding Car Insurance

Car insurance is required by law in most places, and it's an important financial safety net. Here's a breakdown of different types of coverage:

- **Liability Insurance**: This covers costs if you're responsible for injuries or damages to others. It's usually required and includes bodily injury and property damage coverage.
- **Collision Insurance**: This type of insurance covers repairs to your car if you're in an accident, no matter who is at fault. It's especially useful if you have a newer or valuable vehicle.
- **Comprehensive Insurance**: This covers damage from non-collision events, like theft, natural disasters, or vandalism. It's a good idea for added protection, especially in areas prone to weather events.

Additionally, knowing the basics of how insurance works can save you money:

- **Premiums**: Premiums are the regular payments you make to keep your insurance active. These vary based on factors like age, driving record, car type, and where you live.
- **Deductibles**: A deductible is the amount you pay out-of-pocket before insurance kicks in after a claim. Higher deductibles usually mean lower premiums but more out-of-pocket costs if you file a claim. Choose a deductible that you can afford to pay if needed.

- **Filing Claims**: When you need to make a claim, contact your insurer right away. Document the incident, take photos, and gather information like police reports. The insurance company will then process your claim and handle the settlement.

Routine Maintenance Costs

Regular car maintenance helps prevent costly repairs and keeps your car running smoothly. Here are some basic upkeep tips:

- **Oil Changes**: Follow your car's recommended oil change schedule to keep the engine running well. This is one of the most critical maintenance tasks.
- **Tire Rotations and Balancing**: Regularly rotating and balancing your tires helps them wear evenly, making them last longer.
- **Budgeting for Maintenance**: Set aside some money each month for car maintenance costs. This way, when it's time for an oil change or new tires, you're prepared.

Being a smart car owner means keeping an eye on these costs and handling them responsibly. By managing your gas, insurance, and maintenance expenses, you'll save money and make your car ownership experience smoother.

Example Scenarios:

- **Budgeting for Gas:** You've started driving to school every day, and you notice how fast your gas gauge drops. To stay within your budget, you start setting aside a specific amount of your weekly allowance just for fuel. By tracking how much you spend, you'll make your tank last longer and avoid running out of gas money before the weekend.
- **Saving for Car Maintenance:** After your last oil change, you realized car upkeep isn't cheap. So, you start putting a small

amount of money aside each month for regular maintenance like oil changes and tire checks. When the next service comes up, you're ready with enough savings, showing how planning ahead keeps you on the road without stress.

12. Handling Emergencies and Basic First Aid

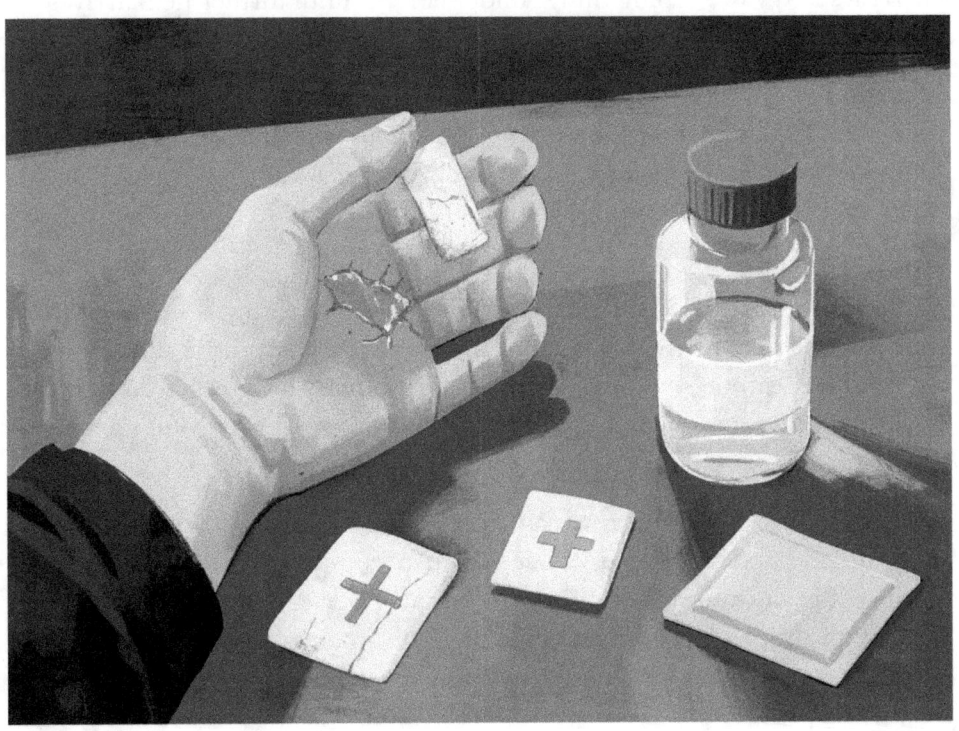

Life can be unpredictable, and knowing how to handle emergencies is an essential skill for everyone. In this chapter, I'll equip you with the knowledge and tools you need to respond effectively to common emergencies, whether it's a minor injury or a more serious situation. I'll cover the basics of first aid for cuts, bruises, and burns, discuss when it's crucial to call for help, and guide you in creating a well-stocked first aid kit. By the end of this chapter, you'll feel more confident and prepared to tackle any situation that comes your way.

1. What to Do in Common Emergencies

Handling common emergencies with calmness and a quick response can make a huge difference, whether it's for yourself or someone nearby. Knowing a few essential steps helps you manage unexpected situations confidently, from minor cuts to more serious incidents. Here's a rundown of what to do in some typical situations where staying composed and knowing the basics is key to keeping things under control until further help arrives.

1. Headaches: Start by drinking water, as dehydration is a common cause. Then go to your room, close the curtains and lie down to rest. Try relaxing your muscles by taking slow, deep breaths. Applying a cold or warm compress to your forehead can also help. If the headache persists, or you experience other symptoms like vision changes, it may be best to seek medical advice.

2. Nosebleeds: Sit down and lean forward slightly. Pinch the soft part of your nose just below the bridge and breathe through your mouth. Hold for ten to fifteen minutes without checking too soon – this gives it time to clot. Avoid leaning back, which can cause blood to go down your throat and make you feel nauseous.

3. Cold and Flu Symptoms: Focus on rest, hydration, and good nutrition to support recovery. Use a warm compress for sinus relief and gargle with salt water to soothe a sore throat. Over-the-counter medications, like cough drops or decongestants, may help manage symptoms. However, if symptoms worsen or if you have trouble breathing, it's important to see a healthcare provider.

4. Sprains and Strains: Use the R.I.C.E. method – Rest, Ice, Compression, and Elevation. Rest the injured part, apply ice for fifteen to twenty minutes at a time (with a cloth in between the ice and skin), use an elastic bandage to compress it, and elevate it to reduce swelling. If there's severe pain or if the injury doesn't improve, it's best to see a doctor.

5. Choking: If someone is choking but can still cough, encourage them to keep coughing to clear the airway. If they can't breathe, talk, or make sounds, step in to help. Place yourself behind them and give them back blows. If that doesn't help, perform the Heimlich maneuver by placing your arms around their waist, and giving quick, inward and upward thrusts just above their belly button. Repeat the abdominal thrusts until the object is out. Call for help if necessary.

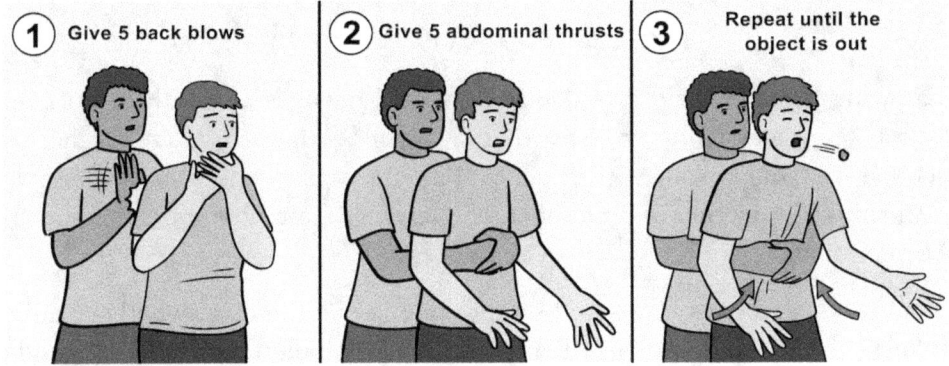

6. Panic Attacks: If you or someone nearby is experiencing a panic attack, focus on slow, deep breathing. Inhale for four counts, hold for four, and exhale for four. Reassure them that they're safe, and encourage them to keep breathing slowly until the panic passes.

Having basic first-aid knowledge can help you stay calm and assist others in emergencies. Always remember to assess the situation first and, when in doubt, call for help.

Example Scenarios:

- **Dealing with a Cut:** You're playing basketball with friends when one of you gets a deep scrape on the knee from a fall. Remember basic first aid steps: rinse the cut with clean water to remove any dirt, pat it dry, and cover it with a bandage to keep it clean. By knowing these simple steps, you help prevent infection and keep the game going.
- **Handling a Sprain:** During gym class, you twist your ankle while running. You know it's a sprain because it's starting to swell and hurt to move. Sit down, elevate your foot, and apply an ice pack for fifteen to twenty minutes to reduce the swelling. By acting quickly and keeping weight off your ankle, you start the healing process right away and avoid making it worse.

2. First Aid Basics: Cuts, Bruises, Burns

Knowing basic first aid for cuts, bruises, and burns is a skill that can help you take quick action in everyday situations, whether you're at home, school, or hanging out with friends. With the right steps, you can handle minor injuries calmly and confidently. Here are some first-aid essentials to keep in mind:

1. Cuts & Scrapes: Cuts and scrapes happen all the time, whether you're biking, playing sports, or just being active. To handle these, start by gently rinsing the wound with cool water to clear out any dirt or debris. Avoid using strong soap directly on the wound – rinse the area around it with mild soap if needed. Once clean, apply a thin layer of antibiotic ointment (like Neosporin) to prevent infection, then cover it with a sterile bandage or gauze. Be sure to change the bandage daily or anytime it gets wet or dirty. Keeping the wound clean and protected will help it heal faster and reduce the chance of infection.

2. Bruises: Bruises can look rough and feel sore, but they're usually not a big deal. A bruise happens when blood vessels under the skin break, often from a fall or impact. If you get a bruise, apply a cold pack or ice wrapped in a cloth (never directly on your skin) to the area for ten to fifteen minutes. This helps reduce swelling and numb the area, making it feel less painful. Avoid massaging the bruise, as this can make it worse. If the bruise is particularly painful or swelling doesn't go down, it's a good idea to get it checked out by an adult.

3. Minor Burns: Minor burns from things like hot objects or steam can be painful but manageable. Start by cooling the burn under cool, running water for ten to fifteen minutes to ease the pain. You can also use a clean, cool, wet cloth if there's no running water nearby. Once the burn has cooled, gently pat it dry and cover it with a sterile, non-stick bandage. Wrap it loosely to avoid putting pressure on the area. Never use ice, butter, or creams on a burn – these can trap heat or cause infection. If the burn blisters, don't pop it, as this increases the risk of infection.

Learning these first aid basics can make a big difference when minor injuries happen. By taking the right steps, you can help prevent infections, reduce pain, and support faster healing.

Example Scenarios:

- **Handling a Bruise:** After bumping into a table corner, you notice a bruise forming on your leg. It's a bit tender and starting to turn purple. Grab an ice pack (or wrap some ice cubes in a cloth) and hold it against the bruise for about ten to fifteen minutes to reduce swelling. By applying ice right away, you keep the bruise from getting worse and help it heal faster.
- **Treating a Minor Burn:** You're helping in the kitchen when you accidentally touch a hot pan, burning your finger. It stings, but you remember to run it under cool (not icy) water for a few minutes to soothe the pain and prevent further skin damage. Pat it dry gently and cover it with a clean, loose bandage. By knowing this first step, you're able to handle the burn safely without panicking.

3. When to Call for Help

Knowing when to call for help can be a real lifesaver, whether you're dealing with an illness, an injury, or another emergency. Sometimes, minor issues can be managed on your own, but in certain situations, getting help is essential. Here's a guide to help you recognize the moments when it's important to reach out to an adult or emergency services:

1. High Fever: If you or someone has a fever over 103°F (39.4°C) or if a mild fever doesn't go down after a few days, it's smart to seek help. High or persistent fevers can indicate serious infections that might need medical treatment.

2. Difficulty Breathing: Having trouble catching your breath, wheezing, or feeling tightness in your chest are signs that something's not right. Breathing issues could signal asthma, allergies, or a respiratory infection, but they could also mean something more serious. In any case, call for help right away to make sure everything's okay.

3. Severe or Persistent Pain: Pain is your body's way of saying something's wrong. Sharp or ongoing pain in your chest, stomach, or head – especially if it comes with nausea, sweating, or dizziness – can mean something serious and needs immediate attention. If you're unsure, it's always better to be safe and reach out for help.

4. Uncontrolled Bleeding: If a wound is bleeding heavily and you can't stop it with gentle pressure, it's time to call for help. Uncontrolled bleeding can lead to shock, and stopping it quickly is essential. Apply firm pressure with a clean cloth and get help as soon as possible.

5. Severe Allergic Reaction: Allergic reactions can be unpredictable. If someone develops swelling, hives, or has difficulty breathing after eating something or being stung, call for help right away. This could be anaphylaxis, which needs immediate medical care.

6. Persistent Vomiting or Diarrhea: If you can't keep any food or liquids down or if you have constant vomiting or diarrhea, dehydration becomes a real risk. When fluids can't stay down, call for assistance – especially if you're feeling dizzy or weak.

7. Major Mental Health Concerns: Feeling overwhelmed, anxious, or hopeless for long periods isn't something to ignore. Talking to an adult, counselor, or healthcare provider can make a big difference. Remember, mental health is just as important as physical health.

Knowing when to get help is an important skill that helps you stay safe. Whether it's calling 911 in a crisis or reaching out to a trusted adult, taking action early can prevent things from getting worse.

EXAMPLE SCENARIOS:

- **Recognizing Severe Pain:** You're playing basketball with friends when you suddenly twist your knee while trying to make a quick move. It hurts for a few minutes, but after a few days, the pain doesn't fade and instead becomes sharp whenever you try to walk. Remembering that persistent pain could signal a serious injury, you ask your parents to take you to the doctor. It's better to be safe and get it checked out rather than hoping it gets better on its own.
- **Experiencing Breathing Difficulties:** During gym class, you notice that your friend is having trouble catching their breath and is

wheezing after running a lap. You can tell something's not right, especially when they start to panic. Instead of waiting, you immediately go to the teacher and let them know your friend needs help. Getting them to the nurse quickly is crucial because breathing issues can escalate fast.

4. Making a Basic First Aid Kit

Creating a basic first aid kit is a smart move for anyone, especially for you teens who are often on the go and might encounter minor injuries or illnesses. Having the right supplies on hand can make a big difference when accidents happen or when someone isn't feeling well. Here's how to build a solid first aid kit with all the essentials to keep at home or in your car:

1. Bandages and Gauze: Stock up on various sizes of adhesive bandages for small cuts and scrapes. Also, include sterile gauze pads and adhesive tape to cover larger wounds.

2. Antiseptic Wipes: These are crucial for cleaning cuts and preventing infections. Make sure to have a good supply to keep everything hygienic.

3. Thermometer: A digital thermometer is essential for checking for fevers. Monitoring temperature is especially important when dealing with illnesses like the flu.

4. Pain Relievers: Keep over-the-counter medications like ibuprofen, acetaminophen, or aspirin. These can help reduce fever and relieve pain.

5. Cold and Flu Medications: Include decongestants, cough suppressants, and throat lozenges to ease symptoms of common colds and flu.

6. Antihistamines: These can be helpful for allergic reactions or when dealing with cold symptoms. They can provide relief from sneezing and runny noses.

7. Hydration Salts: In case of fever or gastrointestinal issues, hydration salts help maintain fluid balance. This is important for recovery.

8. Anti-Diarrheal Medications: These are useful for managing diarrhea, which can happen with various illnesses. Having some on hand is always a good idea.

9. Antacids: Include antacids to relieve upset stomach, heartburn, or acid indigestion. They can provide quick relief when needed.

10. Hand Sanitizer and Disposable Gloves: These are important for keeping everything clean and preventing the spread of germs, especially when someone is sick at home.

Extra Tips for Your Kit

- **Emergency Contact List**: Keep a list of important numbers, including your family doctor, local emergency services, and nearby hospitals. This ensures you have quick access to help if needed.
- **Accessibility and Maintenance**: Store your first aid kit in an easily accessible location, and make it a habit to check it regularly. Replace any expired or used-up items to keep it fully stocked.

Having a well-organized first aid kit is an essential part of being prepared. Whether you're at home or out and about, being equipped to handle minor emergencies can give you peace of mind and confidence. Plus, it shows that you're taking responsibility for your own health and safety. So, gather these supplies, stay organized, and be ready for anything that comes your way!

Example Scenarios:

- **Stocking Up on Essentials:** You're heading out for a camping trip with friends, and you realize that a first aid kit might be helpful. So, before you leave, you gather supplies like adhesive bandages, antiseptic wipes, and pain relievers. You check your home for items like gauze and a thermometer, ensuring everything is in date and ready for any minor injuries that might happen while you're hiking or exploring the outdoors.

- **Emergency Preparedness:** You're playing soccer with friends in the garden when someone takes a hard fall and scrapes their elbow. Thankfully, you have an equipped basic first aid kit at home, including items like antibiotic ointment and extra gauze. You run to grab the kit to clean the wound and apply a bandage, showing your friends how important it is to be ready for accidents.

Conclusion: Moving Forward with Confidence

As you reach the end of this book, it's worth taking a moment to think about the journey you're on and how far you've already come. From learning practical skills like opening a bank account, managing car costs, doing laundry, and building a strong first aid kit, to exploring ways to take care of your health, manage your emotions and find your own voice, you've taken the first steps toward something huge – building the foundation for a confident and successful life. Each topic I've covered here gives you tools to navigate your teenage years and beyond, helping you become the kind of person who can tackle challenges, embrace opportunities, and stand on your own.

Embracing Lifelong Learning

The truth is, learning doesn't end when you finish school or complete a chapter in this book. Real growth and wisdom come from being open to learning throughout your entire life. You'll find that the world is constantly changing, and new skills and knowledge will always be valuable. But lifelong learning doesn't mean just studying harder or taking more classes – it's about being curious and open-minded, willing to pick up new skills, and ready to embrace both success and failure as part of the process.

Whether it's trying out new hobbies, keeping up with new tech, or exploring subjects you're passionate about, make it a habit to learn for the sake of learning. Each new skill, each new piece of information, adds to your confidence and independence. And remember, you don't have to learn everything at once. Skills like financial management, car maintenance, handling relationships, or managing stress will keep evolving with you. As you grow, the things you need to know will change, too. So stay curious, explore topics that interest you, and never be afraid to ask questions. Lifelong learning is a powerful path to independence and self-confidence.

Building Independence and Self-Reliance

As you step into your teenage years, you'll begin making more decisions on your own – decisions that will shape your future. Building independence is about making these choices confidently, based on what you know, what you value, and who you want to become. That's where skills like managing money, staying organized, setting goals, and making sound decisions come into play. Each small step toward independence helps you learn more about yourself, your strengths, and the areas where you can grow.

Independence doesn't mean doing everything by yourself, though. It's okay to ask for help when you need it, whether that's from a friend, family member, or teacher. Self-reliance is about having confidence that you can figure things out and solve problems, even if it means asking for guidance along the way. Taking care of yourself by knowing how to manage stress, stay active, eat well, and maintain good hygiene are all parts of building independence. And remember, being responsible for yourself also means looking out for others – taking action when someone needs help, showing empathy, and being a positive influence on the people around you.

Final Words of Encouragement

As you move forward, remember that you have everything you need within you to succeed. This book has given you a lot of practical advice, but there's one last thing to keep in mind: confidence doesn't mean knowing all the answers. It means believing in your ability to figure things out. There will be times when you make mistakes or face unexpected challenges – that's normal. It's all part of growing up and building a life you can be proud of.

You're already on your way to becoming someone who can handle anything life throws at you. Keep taking those steps, even if they're small, toward the things you want to achieve. You might not always know exactly where you're headed, but trust that each skill you practice, each challenge you overcome, and each piece of advice you put into action will shape you into a more confident, capable person.

So go out there and make the most of what you've learned. Embrace new experiences, enjoy the journey, and keep moving forward with the confidence that you're on the right path. Remember, this isn't just about mastering life skills; it's about becoming the best version of yourself. You've got this!

Thanks for Reading!

I hope you found *Life Skills for Boys – Essential Tips and Skills Every Teenage Boy Should Know!* both practical and motivating as you navigate the journey of growing up and discover your path. My goal was to create a guide that equips you with advice, tools, and confidence to tackle everyday challenges.

As someone who understands how valuable these formative years are, I wanted to share tips that would make life's transitions smoother, from handling relationships and responsibilities to managing daily tasks and self-care. My hope is that this book has inspired you and helped you feel better prepared for whatever life throws your way.

Your feedback is invaluable, both for me as an author and for future readers. If you could take a moment to leave an honest review, it would mean a lot and help others decide if this book is right for them. Please use the QR code below to share your review.

Thank you for choosing *Life Skills for Boys*. Stay curious, stay confident, and always keep learning!

— Sydney Harper

www.ingramcontent.com/pod-product-compliance
Lightning Source LLC
Chambersburg PA
CBHW071212070526
44584CB00019B/3006